CW00457412

Word 2000

Word 2000

Edward Peppitt

QUICK FIX

TEACH YOURSELF BOOKS

For UK orders: please contact Bookpoint Ltd, 130 Milton Park, Abingdon, Oxon OX14 4SB.
Telephone: (44) 01235 400414, Fax: (44) 01235 400454. Lines are open 9.00 - 6.00, Monday
to Saturday, with a 24-hour message answering service. E-mail: orders@bookpoint.co.uk

British Library Cataloguing in Publication Data
A catalogue record for this title is available from the British Library.

First published 2001 by Hodder Headline Plc, 338 Euston Road, London, NW1 3BH.

The 'Teach Yourself' name and logo are registered trade marks of Hodder & Stoughton Ltd.
Computer hardware and software brand names mentioned in this book are protected by their
respective trademarks and are acknowledged.

Typeset by Butford Technical Publishing, Birlingham, Worcs.
Printed in Great Britain for Hodder & Stoughton Educational, a division of
Hodder Headline Plc, 338 Euston Road, London NW1 3BH by Cox & Wyman,
Reading, Berkshire.

Impression number   10 9 8 7 6 5 4 3 2 1
Year   2006 2005   2004   2003   2002   2001

Contents

Getting Started

Start Word 2000

1 Click **Start**.

2 Point to **Programs**.

3 Select **Microsoft Word**.

OR

Double-click on your desktop.

Word 2000

Close Word 2000

Click on **X** in top right-hand corner of screen

OR

1 In the **File** menu, select **Exit**.

2 Save your document(s) if you are prompted to do so.

Move around text using the keyboard

There are four keystroke combinations that will enable you to navigate around a document quickly.

[Ctrl] + [Home] takes you straight to the beginning of the document.

[Ctrl] + [End] takes you straight to the end of the document.

[Ctrl] + [Pg Up] takes you to the top of the preceding page.

[Ctrl] + [Pg Dn] takes you to the top of the next page.

Use keyboard shortcuts

There are keyboard shortcuts for most of the common commands in Word. We have chosen not to list the keyboard equivalent for all the instructions in this book, but you can learn many of the shortcuts by looking through the drop-down main menus.

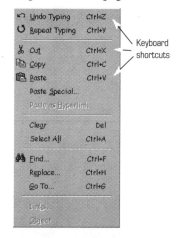

Keyboard shortcuts

Use scrollbars

Scrollbars provide another means of navigating through a document.

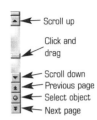

Scroll up
Click and drag
Scroll down
Previous page
Select object
Next page

Set file properties

You can set file properties to make it easier to find or sort documents at a later date.

1 In the **File** menu, select **Properties**.

2 You can summarize your document by entering data for title, subject, categories, keywords and comments.

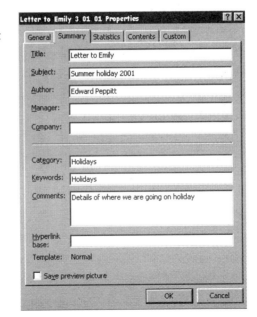

Letter to Emily 3.01.01 Properties

General | Summary | Statistics | Contents | Custom

Title: Letter to Emily
Subject: Summer holiday 2001
Author: Edward Peppitt
Manager:
Company:

Category: Holidays
Keywords: Holidays
Comments: Details of where we are going on holiday

Hyperlink base:
Template: Normal

☐ Save preview picture

OK | Cancel

Replace text by highlighting

1 Highlight the text that you want to replace.

2 Type in the new text.

Replace text using Overtype

1 Move cursor to where you want to replace text.

2 Double-click OVR on the status bar.

3 Start typing. As you type, the text ahead will be overwritten.

Delete single character

1 To delete the character to the right of the cursor, press **[Del]**.

2 To delete the character to the left, press **[Backspace]**.

Delete text

1 Highlight the text that you want to delete.

2 Press the **[Del]** key or the **[Backspace]** key.

Screen Display

Change the way a document is displayed

Word offers a number of ways of viewing your document.

Click on the appropriate icon in the bottom left-hand corner of your screen.

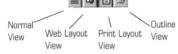

Normal View / Web Layout View / Print Layout View / Outline View

Display toolbars

1 In the **View** menu, select **Toolbars**.

2 Click on any toolbar name to display it.

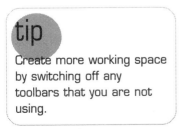

tip

Create more working space by switching off any toolbars that you are not using.

- ✓ Standard
- ✓ Formatting
- AutoText
- Clipboard
- Control Toolbox
- Database
- ✓ Drawing
- Forms
- Frames
- Picture
- Reviewing
- Tables and Borders
- Visual Basic
- Web
- Web Tools
- WordArt
- Customize...

Display ruler

In the **View** menu, select **Ruler**.

Switch to full screen display

To create more working space, switch to full screen display. All toolbars and menus are hidden from view, devoting the full screen to your working document.

1 In the **View** menu, select **Full Screen**.

2 Click **Close Full Screen** to revert to previous view.

Use Zoom

The Zoom facility allows you to alter the size of the document as it is displayed on your screen. It does not alter the final printed document.

1 In the **View** menu, select **Zoom**.

2 Choose a Zoom option.

3 Click **OK**.

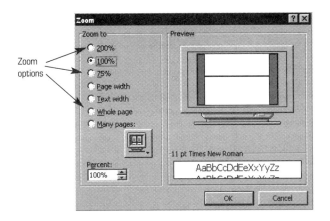

Turn on/off dynamic menus

In Word 2000, each drop-down menu only displays the most commonly used options for the first few seconds. After a brief pause, menus expand automatically to show all available commands.

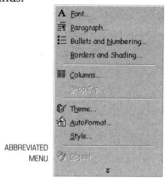

ABBREVIATED
MENU

EXPANDED
MENU

You can switch this facility off.

1 In the **Tools** menu, select **Customize**.

2 Click on **Options** tab.

3 Remove the tick as indicated opposite.

4 Click **Close**.

Turn on/off dynamic toolbars

Word 2000 saves desktop space by combining two or more toolbars on a single line, and displaying only those icons that are commonly used.

You can switch this facility off.

1 In the **Tools** menu, select **Customize**.

2 Click on **Options** tab.

3 Remove the tick where indicated.

4 Click **Close**.

Remove tick from this box to turn off dynamic toolbars

Remove tick from this box to turn off dynamic menus

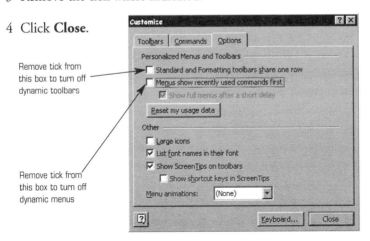

Customize

Toolbars | Commands | Options

Personalized Menus and Toolbars

☐ Standard and Formatting toolbars share one row

☐ Menus show recently used commands first

☑ Show full menus after a short delay

Reset my usage data

Other

☐ Large icons

☑ List font names in their font

☑ Show ScreenTips on toolbars

☐ Show shortcut keys in ScreenTips

Menu animations: (None)

Keyboard... | Close

Creating Documents

Create a new blank document

1 Start Word.

2 A new blank document will appear automatically.

OR

1 Click **Start**.

2 Select **New Office Document**.

3 Select **Blank document**.

4 Click **OK**.

New Office Document

Open Office Document

Windows Update

WinZip

Programs

Favorites

Documents

Settings

Find

Help

Run...

Log Off Edward Peppitt...

Shut Down...

Start

Create a new document using a template

1 Start Word.

2 In the **File** menu, select **New**.

3 Click on the tab for the type of document you want to create.

4 Select a template.

5 Click **OK**.

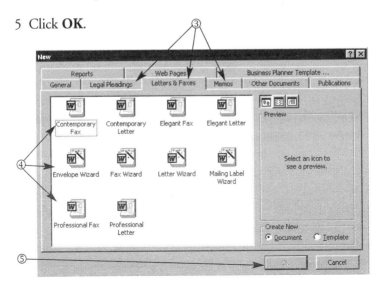

Create a letter using Letter Wizard

1 Start Word.

2 Open a new blank document, or another suitable document template.

3 In the **Tools** menu, select **Letter Wizard**.

4 Follow the wizard's step-by-step instructions.

5 Click **OK**.

6 When the wizard has finished, you can amend or adjust the letter to suit your requirements.

Work through each tab in turn

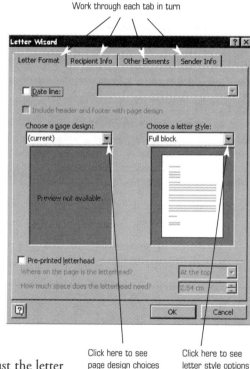

Click here to see page design choices

Click here to see letter style options

Create new documents using wizards

1 Start Word.

2 In the **File** menu, select **New**.

3 Click the tab containing the wizard you want to use.

4 Click to select the wizard.

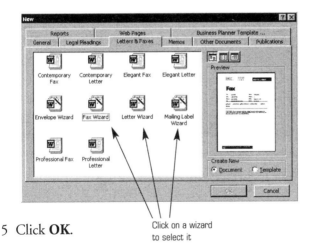

5 Click **OK**.

Click on a wizard
to select it

6 Follow the wizard's step-by-step instructions to create your document.

Saving Documents

Save a document for the first time

1 Click 🖫 on the standard toolbar.

2 Navigate to the folder where you wish to store the document.

3 Give the document a meaningful name.

4 Click **Save**.

Save a document again

You should remember to save your document at regular intervals in one of the following ways:

- Click 🖫 at any time.

- In the **File** menu, select **Save**.

- Hold down **[Ctrl]** and press **[S]**.

Save a document as a different file type

1 In the **File** menu, select **Save As**.

2 Click on down arrow next to **Save as type**.

3 Select appropriate file type.

4 Click **Save**.

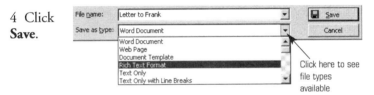

File name:	Letter to Frank		💾 Save
Save as type:	Word Document	▾	Cancel
	Word Document		
	Web Page		
	Document Template		
	Rich Text Format		Click here to see
	Text Only		file types
	Text Only with Line Breaks		available

Save a copy of a document

1 Open the document that you want to copy.

2 In the **File** menu, select **Save As**.

3 Navigate to the directory where you want to store the copy.

4 Rename the document.

5 Click **Save**.

Opening Documents

Open a document

1 Click .

   OR

   In the **File** menu, select **Open**.

2 Navigate to the folder containing the document you want to open.

3 Double-click on the document.

   OR

   Click once on the document and then click 📂 Open ▾.

---

tip

If you want to open a document that you have worked on recently, you may see it listed at the foot of the File menu. If so, just click on it.

Find a document

It is very easy to forget where on your hard disk you have saved a document. If this happens to you:

1 Click **Start** and select **Find**, then **Files** or **Folders**.

2 Enter the name of the document, or a part of it.

3 Add any other data that might assist the search process into the appropriate fields (e.g. a date range or some keywords contained in the text).

4 Click **Find Now**.

5 Files matching the search criteria will be listed.

6 Double-click on the file name to open it.

Find: Files named Watson

File   Edit   View   Options   Help

Name & Location | Date | Advanced

Named: Watson

Containing text:

Look in: My Documents

☑ Include subfolders   Browse...

[Find Now]   [Stop]   [New Search]

Name	In Folder
Watson, Fred 31.5.00	D:\My Documents\Sample Requests
Watson, Barry 4.7.00	D:\My Documents\Sample Requests

2 file(s) found   Monitoring New Items

Printing Documents

Print a whole document

Click 🖨️ **OR** Hold down **[Ctrl]** and press **[P]**.

Print part of a document

1 In the **File** menu, select **Print**.

2 Select **Page range**.

3 Click **OK**.

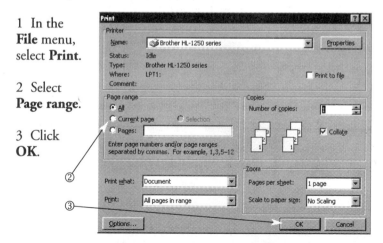

Change print criteria

In the **File** menu, select **Print**. You can:

- Select print range.

- Specify number of copies to print.

- Select scale or zoom.

- Select odd or even pages only.

Switch to a different printer

1 In the **File** menu, select **Print**.

2 Click on down arrow next to **Printer Name**.

3 Select printer.

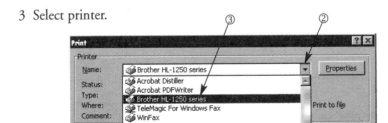

Edit printer properties

1 In the **File** menu, select **Print**.

2 Click on **Properties**.

3 Select desired options.

4 Click **OK**.

Click on each tab to see
more printer properties

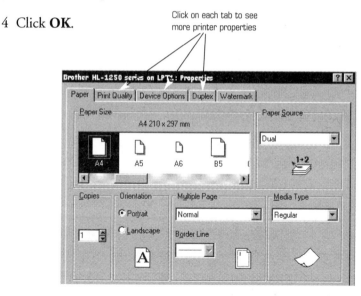

Preview a document before printing

1 Click 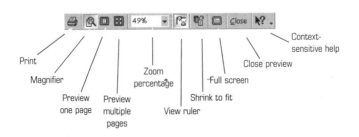.

   OR

   In the **File** menu, select **Print Preview**.

2 Click **Close** to return to the previous view.

Adjust print preview settings

1 Select the appropriate option from the Print Preview toolbar.

2 Use the scrollbar to navigate between previewed pages.

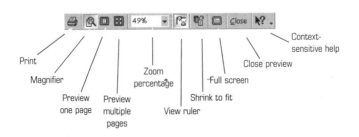

Print

Magnifier

Preview one page

Preview multiple pages

Zoom percentage

View ruler

Shrink to fit

Full screen

Close preview

Context-sensitive help

Alter the page setup

1 In the **File** menu, select **Page Setup**.

2 Alter paper size, paper source, layout and margins as required.

3 Click **OK** when finished.

PAPER SIZE
SETUP

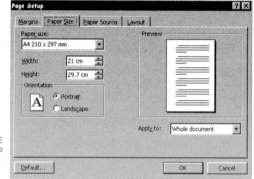

PAPER SOURCE
SETUP

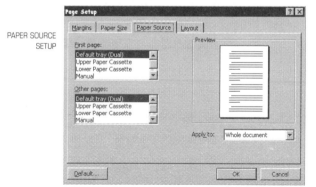

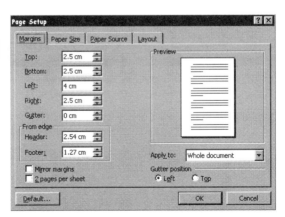

LAYOUT
SETUP

Page Setup

Margins | Paper Size | Paper Source | **Layout**

Section start:

New page

Headers and footers
☐ Different odd and even
☐ Different first page

Vertical alignment:

Top

☐ Suppress endnotes

Line Numbers...

Borders...

Preview

Apply to: Whole document

Default...   OK   Cancel

MARGINS
SETUP

Page Setup

Margins | Paper Size | Paper Source | Layout

Top: 2.5 cm

Bottom: 2.5 cm

Left: 4 cm

Right: 2.5 cm

Gutter: 0 cm

From edge

Header: 2.54 cm

Footer: 1.27 cm

☐ Mirror margins
☐ 2 pages per sheet

Preview

Apply to: Whole document

Gutter position
◉ Left   ○ Top

Default...   OK   Cancel

Address an envelope

If your printer allows you to feed envelopes through it then you can print an address directly onto the envelope.

1 In the **Tools** menu, select **Envelopes and Labels**.

2 Click to select the **Envelopes** tab.

3 Enter the delivery address if it does not appear automatically.

4 Enter a return address if applicable.

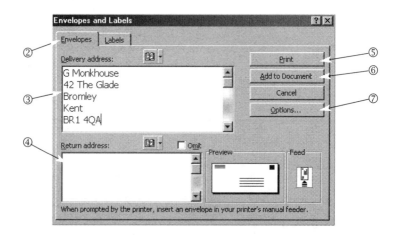

5 Click **Print** if you want to print the envelope on its own.

6 Click **Add to Document** if you want to print the envelope at the same time as the complete document.

7 Click **Options** to change the envelope printing options.

8 Click to select the **Envelope Options** tab.

9 Make changes as desired.

10 Click **OK**.

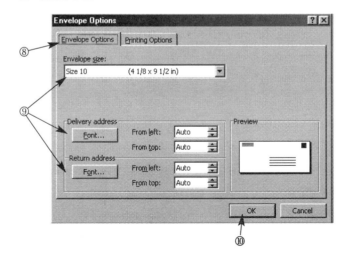

Print two pages on a single sheet

1 In the **File** menu, select **Page Setup**.

2 Click to select the **Margins** tab.

3 Click to select **2 Pages Per Sheet**.

4 Click **OK**.

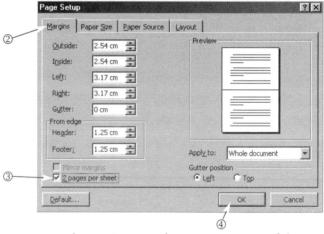

When you are ready to print your document, use any of the
normal printing methods.

Print multiple pages on a single sheet

In Word 2000, you can print thumbnails of the pages of a document on a single sheet.

1 In the **File** menu, select **Print**.

2 Click to select the desired number of pages per sheet.

3 Click **OK**.

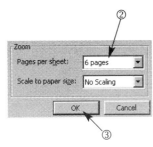

Shrink text to fit a single page

Sometimes a document will not quite fit onto a single page. Word can automatically shrink the document so that it fits neatly onto a single page.

1 Click 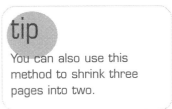.

2 Click.

3 Click **Close**.

tip
You can also use this method to shrink three pages into two.

Moving, Copying and Pasting

Select text using the mouse

To select a word, double-click the word.

To select a range of text, click and hold while dragging mouse over the text.

To select a line:

1 Move mouse into left margin until cursor changes to inward-pointing arrow.

2 Click once.

To select a paragraph:

1 Move mouse into left margin until cursor changes to inward-pointing arrow.

2 Click twice.

To select all the text:

1 Move mouse into left margin until cursor changes to inward-pointing arrow.

2 Click three times.

Deselect text

Click anywhere within the text

OR

Press one of the arrow keys.

Drag and drop text (move)

You can move text around a document using the drag and drop feature:

1 Highlight text to be moved.

2 Click on highlighted text and move to desired position.

3 Release mouse.

Drag and drop text (copy)

1 Highlight text to be copied.

2 Hold down **[Ctrl]** key, click on highlighted text and move to desired position.

3 Release mouse.

Cut text

1 Highlight text to be cut.

2 Click ✂ .

Copy text

1 Highlight text to be copied.

2 Click 📋 .

Paste text

1 Move cursor to where text will be inserted.

2 Click 📋 .

tip

There are keyboard shortcuts to make cut, copy and paste even quicker:

[Ctrl] and [X] = cut

[Ctrl] and [C] = copy

[Ctrl] and [V] = paste

Make two or more copy selections

1 In the **View** menu, point to **Toolbars** and select **Clipboard**.

2 Highlight first copy selection, then click in the Clipboard toolbar.

3 Highlight next copy selection, then click in the Clipboard toolbar.

4 You can make up to twelve copy selections in this way.

5 Now:

• Click 🛍 Paste All to paste all selections in the same place.

   OR

• Click on appropriate Word icon to paste single selection.

tip

You can also use the Office Clipboard to copy content between Microsoft Office software applications.

Formatting

Set character spacing

1 Highlight the characters or words that you want to space.

2 In the **Format** menu, select **Font**.

3 Click on
Character Spacing.

4 Select appropriate character spacing and position.

Character spacing

Character position

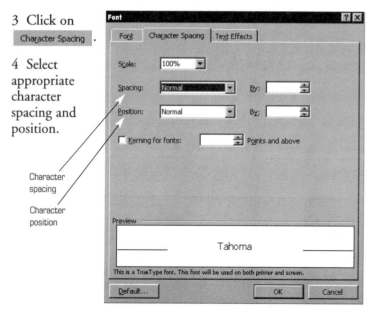

Set line/paragraph spacing

1 Highlight the lines or paragraphs that you want to space.

2 In the **Format** menu, select **Paragraph**.

3 Make a selection in the **Line spacing** field.

Select line spacing

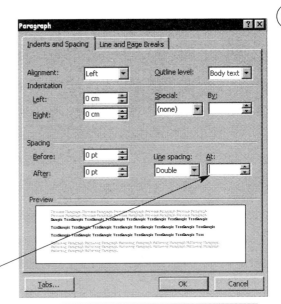

Paragraph ? X

Indents and Spacing | **Line and Page Breaks**

Alignment: [Left ▾]   Outline level: [Body text ▾]

Indentation
Left: [0 cm ▲▼]   Special: [(none) ▾]   By: [▲▼]
Right: [0 cm ▲▼]

Spacing
Before: [0 pt ▲▼]   Line spacing: [Double ▾]   At: [▲▼]
After: [0 pt ▲▼]

Preview

[Tabs...]   [OK]   [Cancel]

tip

There are keyboard shortcuts to make setting line spacing quicker. After you have highlighted the lines to be spaced, hold down [Ctrl] and press [1] (for single line spacing), [2] (for double line spacing) and so on.

Use bold/italic/underline

1 Highlight the text that you want to change.

2 Click on the appropriate icon in the formatting toolbar.

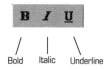

Bold   Italic   Underline

You can set bold, italic or underline as you type:

1 Move cursor to the point where you want to type.

2 Click on the appropriate icon in the formatting toolbar.

3 Begin typing.

Change typeface/font or text size

1 Highlight the text that you want to change.

2 Select an appropriate font or typeface from the drop-down menus.

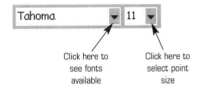

Click here to
see fonts
available

Click here to
select point
size

tip

If you want to incorporate a number of different typefaces
and text sizes, you may find it easier to introduce a document
style into your documents (see page 212).

Change font formatting

FORMATTING

There are other changes you can make to the way text looks:

1 Highlight the text that you want to change.

2 In the **Format** menu, select **Font**.

3 Make the appropriate changes and click **OK**.

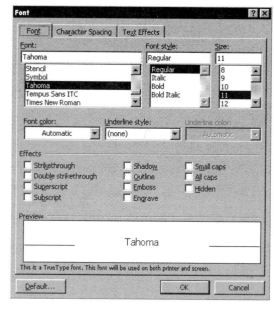

You can alter the font, font style and size. You can set simple effects, like a text shadow or outline. Click on **Text Effects** to set other special effects like text that blinks or sparkles.

Align text

1 Highlight the text that you want to align.

2 Click on the appropriate icon in the formatting toolbar.

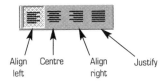

Align   Centre   Align   Justify
left   right

Align text as you type

1 Move cursor to the point where you want to type.

2 Click on the appropriate icon in the formatting toolbar.

3 Text will be aligned accordingly from this point forward.

Copy formatting/use format painter

The format painter allows you to copy the formatting of a word, sentence or paragraph and apply it to another part of a document.

1 Highlight the words or characters whose formatting you want to copy.

2 Click .

3 Click and drag mouse over the text that you want to format.

4 Release mouse.

You can copy the formatting for an entire paragraph:

1 Click ¶ .

2 Highlight the paragraph mark at the end of the paragraph whose formatting you want to copy.

3 Click .

4 Click and drag mouse over paragraph mark at the end of the paragraph that you want to format.

5 Release mouse.

Set up AutoFormat

Word can format your document automatically. There are a number of AutoFormat options that you can set up.

1 In the **Tools** menu, select **AutoCorrect**.

2 Click on the **AutoFormat** tab.

3 Select appropriate AutoFormat options.

4 Click **OK**.

Select AutoFormat options

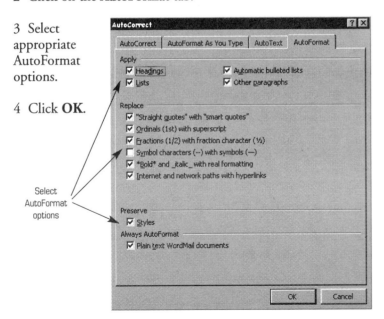

Apply AutoFormat to whole document

1 In the **Format** menu, select **AutoFormat**.

2 To be safe, select
**AutoFormat and review each
change**.

3 Select a document type,
and click **OK**.

4 Scroll through formatted
document to see how it looks.

5 To undo all formatting changes, select **Reject all**.

To accept all formatting changes, select **Accept**.

To consider each change individually, select **Review Changes**.

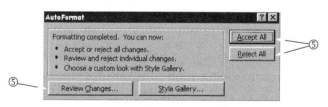

Apply AutoFormat to part of a document

1 Highlight the text that you want to AutoFormat.

2 Repeat steps 1–5 above.

Review AutoFormat changes

You may wish to keep some AutoFormat changes, and reject others:

1 Click **Review Changes** at the end of the Auto-Format procedure.

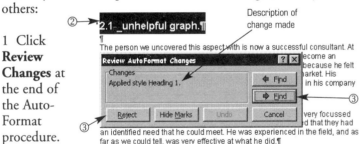

2 A dialog box appears summarizing each change in turn, with the relevant change highlighted in the text.

3 For each change either choose **Reject** or click on to accept it and move to the next one.

Format a document automatically as you type

1 In the **Tools** menu, select **AutoCorrect**.

2 Click on the **AutoFormat As You Type** tab.

3 Select from the AutoFormat options available.

4 Click **OK**.

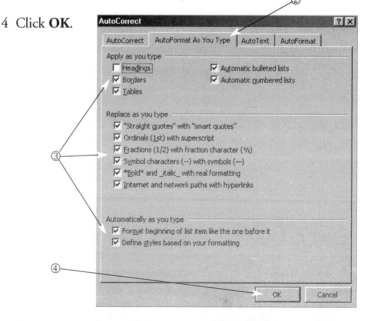

Turn on Click and Type

Click and Type is a feature in Word that allows you to type text anywhere on a page, not just at the start of a line.

1 In the **Tools** menu, select **Options**.

2 Click on the **Edit** tab.

3 Click on **Enable Click and Type** check box.

4 Click **OK**.

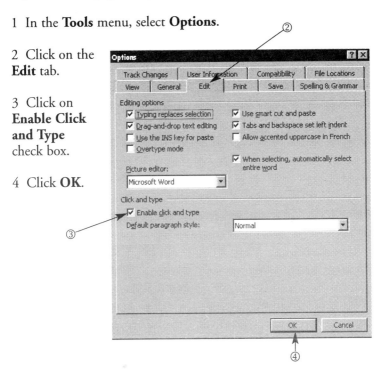

Use Click and Type

1 Switch to Print Layout View or Web Layout View.

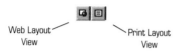

Web Layout View — Print Layout View

2 Move cursor to a blank area where you want to insert text or a graphic.

3 Click to activate the Click and Type pointer.

4 Double-click, and then start typing.

Change the case of text

1 Highlight the text whose case you want to change.

2 In the **Format** menu, select **Change Case**.

3 Make appropriate selection.

4 Click **OK**.

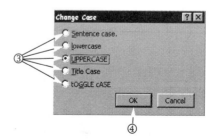

Keep lines of text together on a page

1 Highlight the lines of text that you want to keep together.

2 In the **Format** menu, select **Paragraph**.

3 Click on the **Line and Page Breaks** tab.

Click here to keep paragraphs together

4 Select **Keep lines together**.

5 Click **OK**.

Click here to keep lines together

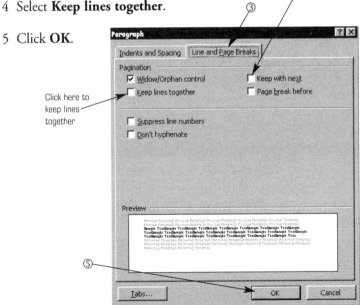

Keep paragraphs together

1 Highlight the lines of text that you want to keep together.

2 In the **Format** menu, select **Paragraph**.

3 Click on the **Line and Page Breaks** tab.

4 Select **Keep with next**.

5 Click **OK**.

Delete text

1 Highlight text that you want to delete.

2 Press the **[Del]** key.

Insert a dropped capital

1 Click to the right of the capital letter that you want to drop.

2 In the **Format** menu, select **Drop Cap**.

3 Select the
position of the
dropped capital.

4 Select any of the
other options
available.

5 Click **OK**.

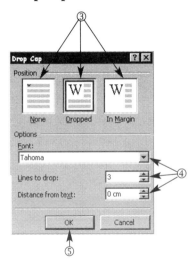

EXAMPLE OF A
PARAGRAPH WITH A
DROPPED CAPITAL

When we fed this piece of analysis back to the client, initially he rejected it. We then explored the question, "if we take the proposition as true, does your behaviour make sense?" He agreed with this in a thoughtful way.
We then searched for any other basis, which would completely explain his behaviour. We found none.

Hyphenate words automatically

Word can hyphenate words automatically to make lines in a paragraph of text more even.

1 In the **Tools** menu, point to **Language** and select **Hyphenation**.

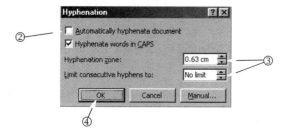

2 Click to select **Automatically hyphenate document**.

3 Make other changes to hyphenation settings as appropriate.

4 Click **OK**.

Hyphenate words manually

1 In the **Tools** menu, point to **Language** and select
Hyphenation.

2 Set appropriate hyphenation zone.

3 Limit the number of consecutive hyphens as appropriate.

4 Click **Manual**.

Word will display each proposed hyphen in turn:

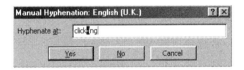

- Click **Yes** to accept the proposed hyphen.

- Click **No** to reject the proposed hyphen.

- Click at a new point inside the word to hyphenate it
differently.

Set Widows and Orphans control

Sometimes a single line from a paragraph ends up on its own on the next page. You can use the widow/orphan control to make sure that this does not happen.

1 Highlight the paragraph.

2 In the **Format** menu, select **Paragraph**.

3 Click to select the **Line and Page Breaks** tab.

4 Click to select **Widow/Orphan control**.

5 Click **OK**.

Paragraph dialog box:

Indents and Spacing | Line and Page Breaks

Pagination
- ☑ Widow/Orphan control
- ☐ Keep lines together
- ☐ Keep with next
- ☐ Page break before

- ☐ Suppress line numbers
- ☐ Don't hyphenate

Preview

Tabs... | OK | Cancel

View format settings for a paragraph

1 In the **Help** menu, select **What's This?**

2 Click the text whose formatting you want to view.

3 A summary information box appears.

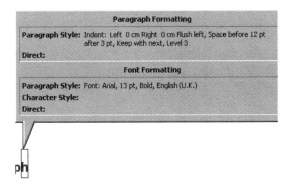

Margins

Set left/right margins with ruler

1 In the **View** menu, select **Ruler**.

2 Change display to Print Layout View. The shaded parts of the ruler indicate the left and right margins.

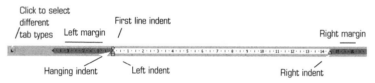

Click to select
different
/tab types   Left margin   First line indent /   Right margin

Hanging indent   Left indent   Right indent

3 Move mouse pointer to the left or right end of the white part of the ruler. The mouse pointer will change into a twin-headed arrow.

4 Click and drag the margin to the desired position.

5 Release mouse.

Dotted line appears when dragging margin to new position

Set top/bottom margin using ruler

1 In the **View** menu, select **Ruler**.

2 Change display to Print Layout View. The shaded parts of the ruler on the left-hand side of the screen indicate the top and bottom margins.

3 Move mouse pointer to the top or bottom end of the white part of the ruler. The mouse pointer will change into a twin-headed arrow.

4 Click and drag the margin to the desired position.

5 Release mouse.

Click to select different tab types

Top margin

Set margins using a dialog box

1 In the **File** menu, select **Page Setup**.

2 Click on the **Margins** tab.

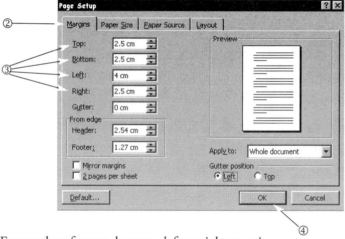

3 Enter values for top, bottom, left or right margins.

4 Click **OK**.

Create a hanging indent

A hanging indent is when all the lines in a paragraph are
indented apart from the first one.

1 In the **View** menu, select **Ruler**.

2 Change display to Print Layout View.

3 Click anywhere inside the paragraph in which you want to
add a hanging indent.

4 Click on hanging indent marker and drag to desired position.

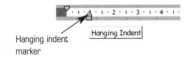

Hanging indent
marker

5 Release mouse.

Indent the first line of a paragraph

1 In the **View** menu, select **Ruler**.

2 Change display to Print Layout View.

3 Click anywhere inside the paragraph in which you want a first line indent.

4 Click on first line indent marker and drag to desired position.

First line indent
marker

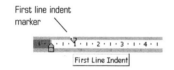

5 Release mouse.

Indent all the lines of a paragraph

1 In the **View** menu, select **Ruler**.

2 Change display to Print Layout View.

3 Click anywhere inside the paragraph that you want to indent.

4 Click on left indent marker and drag to desired position.

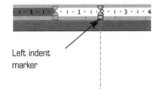

Left indent
marker

5 Release mouse.

Indent lines using the menu

1 Highlight the text that you want to indent.

2 In the **Format** menu, select **Paragraph**.

3 Click on **Indents and Spacing** tab.

4 Enter desired
indent values.

5 Click **OK**.

Paragraph	? x

③

Indents and Spacing | Line and Page Breaks

Alignment: [Left ▾]   Outline level: [Body text ▾]

Indentation

④ → Left: [0 cm ⬍]   Special: [(none) ▾]   By: [⬍]

Right: [0 cm ⬍]

Spacing

Before: [0 pt ⬍]

After: [0 pt ⬍]   Line spacing: [Single ▾]   At: [⬍]

Preview

[Tabs...]   [OK]   [Cancel]

⑤

Indent right-hand edge of paragraph

1 In the **View** menu, select **Ruler**.

2 Change display to Print Layout View.

3 Click anywhere inside the paragraph that you want to indent.

4 Click on right indent marker and drag to desired position.

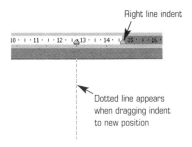

Right line indent

Dotted line appears
when dragging indent
to new position

5 Release mouse.

Tabs

Change default tab stops

By default, Word has tab stops set at intervals of 1.27 cm (about half an inch). Every time you press **[Tab]** the cursor moves 1.27 cm to the next tab stop.

You can change the default tab stop settings.

1 In the **Format** menu, select **Tabs**.

2 Enter a new value in the **Default tab stops** field.

3 Click **OK**.

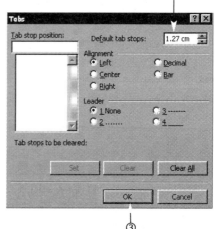

Use custom tab stops

Tabs help you to control the alignment of text in a document. There are four types of tab stops.

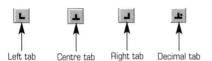

Left tab   Centre tab   Right tab   Decimal tab

1 Click the tab symbol until you see the tab that you want.

2 Move mouse pointer to the ruler, and click and hold where you want the tab. A vertical line will appear through your document, indicating where the tab will appear.

3 Drag mouse to the left or right until the tab is in the desired position.

4 Release mouse.

Move a custom tab stop

1 Point at the tab stop symbol in the toolbar.

2 Click and drag tab stop to new position.

3 Release mouse.

Delete a custom tab stop

1 Point at the tab stop symbol in the toolbar.

2 Click and drag symbol away from the ruler.

3 Release mouse.

Line up rows of figures by their decimal point

1 Highlight the rows of figures to line up.

2 Click on the tab symbol until 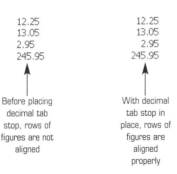 appears.

3 Place tab stop at appropriate place in the ruler.

4 Click at start of each row of figures.

5 Press **[Tab]** once.

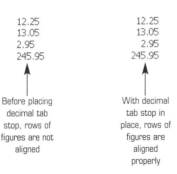

12.25	12.25
13.05	13.05
2.95	2.95
245.95	245.95

Before placing decimal tab stop, rows of figures are not aligned

With decimal tab stop in place, rows of figures are aligned properly

Set precise measurements for tabs

1 In the **Format** menu, select **Tabs**.

2 Enter a value in the **Tab stop position** field.

3 Select appropriate alignment.

4 Click **OK**.

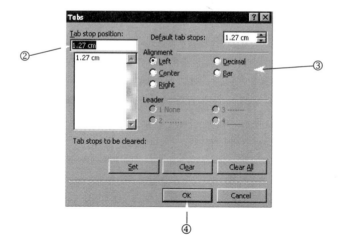

Set tab stops with leader characters

1 Highlight the paragraph in which you want tab stops with leader characters.

2 In the **Format** menu, select **Tabs**.

3 In the **Tab stop position** field, enter a value for a new tab or select an existing one.

4 Click desired leader type.

5 Click **Set**.

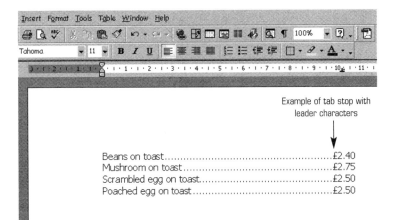

Example of tab stop with leader characters

Headers and Footers

Add page numbers

Word can
automatically
number the pages
of your document.

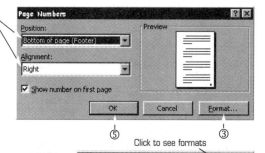

1 In the **Insert**
menu, select **Page
Numbers**.

2 Select where the numbers
should be positioned, and how
they should be aligned.

3 Click on **Format** to see other
page numbering options.

Click to see formats

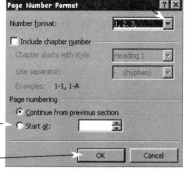

4 Click **OK**.

You can start page
numbering at a
particular page

5 Click **OK**.

Add a header (running head)

1 In the **View** menu, select **Header and Footer**.

2 Type an appropriate running head where indicated.

3 Highlight the running head and apply any formatting (e.g. font settings) you require.

4 Click **Close**.

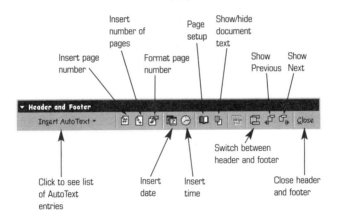

Add a footer

1 In the **View** menu, select **Header and Footer**.

2 Click on 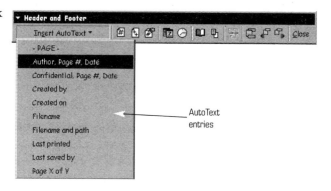 to move cursor from header to footer area.

3 Type appropriate footer text, or select an appropriate AutoText entry.

4 Click **Close**.

| Header and Footer |
| Insert AutoText ▾ |

- PAGE -
Author, Page #, Date
Confidential, Page #, Date
Created by
Created on
Filename
Filename and path
Last printed
Last saved by
Page X of Y

AutoText entries

tip

AutoText entries, such as page number, are automatically updated as your document changes. So AutoText entries are always more efficient than manual ones.

Remove a header or footer

1 In the **View** menu, select **Header and Footer**.

2 Select the text in the header or footer that you want to remove.

3 Press **[Del]**.

Specify different headers and footers

Often you want a different running head on odd and even pages.

1 In the **File** menu, select **Page Setup**.

2 Click on the **Layout** tab.

3 Below **Headers and footers**, place a tick in **Different odd and even**.

4 Place a tick in **Different first page** if the first page of your document will have its own header/footer.

5 Click **OK**.

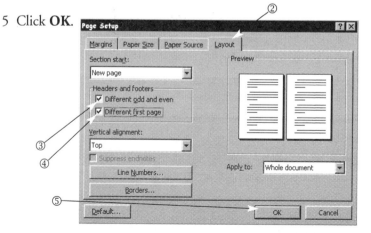

Specify first page header or footer

1 Move cursor to start of document.

2 In the **View** menu, select **Header and Footer**.

3 Enter first page **Header** text.

4 Click on ![icon] to move cursor to first page footer.

5 Enter first page **Footer** text.

6 Click **Close**.

Specify even page header or footer

1 Move cursor to first even page of document.

2 In the **View** menu, select **Header and Footer**.

3 Enter even page **Header** text.

4 Click on to move cursor to even page footer.

5 Enter even page **Footer** text.

6 Click **Close**.

Specify odd page header or footer

1 Move cursor to first odd page of document.

2 In the **View** menu, select **Header and Footer**.

3 Enter odd page **Header** text.

4 Click on 🖳 to move cursor to odd page footer.

5 Enter odd page **Footer** text.

6 Click **Close**.

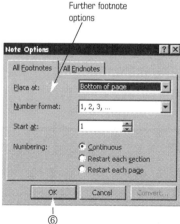

Add a footnote

1 Move cursor to where you want the footnote mark to appear.

2 In the **Insert** menu, select **Footnote**.

3 Select **Footnote**.

4 Choose a numbering style.

5 Click on **Options** for further footnote options.

6 Click **OK**.

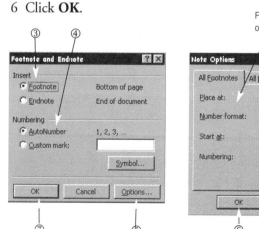

7 Click **OK**.

8 Type the text that you want to appear in the footnote.

9 Double-click on footnote number to return to that point in the document.

In the echo chamber
of my mind,
your voice still whispers[1]
lyrics of a sweeter,
more lovely song.

(29/8/98)

[1] Compare with Flicker Flame (Sept 97)

Example of
a footnote

Add an endnote

An endnote is identical to a footnote, except that all the notes appear together at the end of the document, rather than on each page.

1 Repeat steps 1 and 2 on page 74.

2 Select **Endnote**.

3 Repeat steps 4–8 on page 74.

Edit a footnote or endnote

1 Move cursor over appropriate footnote marker within the text.

2 Double-click to move cursor straight to the footnote or endnote text.

3 Make appropriate corrections.

4 Double-click on the footnote number to move cursor back to the place where you inserted the footnote mark.

tip

If you have Tooltips switched on, you will find that the footnote text appears in a caption bubble whenever you move your mouse over a footnote or endnote marker.

Insert a cross-reference

1 Enter the text that you want to accompany your cross-reference.

2 In the **Insert** menu, select **Cross-reference**.

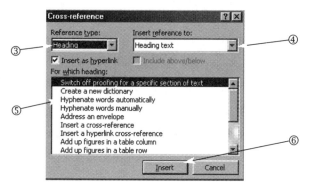

3 Select an appropriate **Reference type**.

4 Select an appropriate reference insertion point.

5 Click to select the cross-reference.

6 Click **Insert**.

7 Click **Close**.

Insert a hyperlink cross-reference

1 Enter the text that you want to accompany your cross-reference.

2 In the **Insert** menu, select **Cross-reference**.

3 Select an appropriate **Reference type**.

4 Select an appropriate reference insertion point.

5 Click to select the cross-reference.

6 Click to select **Insert as hyperlink**.

7 Click **Insert**.

8 Click **Close**.

Proofing Tools

Check spelling and grammar as you type

1 In the **Tools** menu, select **Options**.

2 Click on the **Spelling & Grammar** tab.

3 Place a tick in **Check spelling as you type**.

4 Select any other spelling or grammar options.

5 Click **OK**.

From now on, Word will automatically place a wavy red line under words that it does not recognize, and a wavy green line under common grammatical errors.

Correct spelling or grammar

1 Right-click on a wavy red or green line.

2 Select the appropriate correction.

   OR

   Select **Ignore** (to keep the word as spelled in the document).

   OR

   Select **Add** (to add the word to the computer's dictionary).

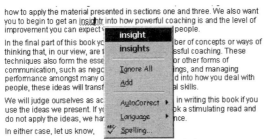

how to apply the material presented in sections one and three. We also want you to begin to get an insight into how powerful coaching is and the level of improvement you can expect ▯ ▯ people.

In the final part of this book y▯ ▯ber of concepts or ways of thinking that, in our view, are ▯ ▯ssful coaching. These techniques also form the esse▯ ▯r other forms of communication, such as nego▯ ▯ngs, and managing performance amongst many o▯ ▯d into how you deal with people, these ideas will transf▯ ▯al skills.

We will judge ourselves as ac▯ ▯ in writing this book if you use the ideas we present. If y▯ ▯k a stimulating read and do not apply the ideas, we ha▯ ▯nce.

In either case, let us know, ▯

At the end of this book, you will find many ways to contact us.

Menu items shown in the image:

- insight
- insights
- Ignore All
- Add
- AutoCorrect ▶
- Language ▶
- Spelling...

Correct spelling and grammar in a complete document

1 Click ![ABC check icon].

OR

In the **Tools** menu, select **Spelling and Grammar**.

2 Select an appropriate response to each error found.

3 Click **OK** when spelling check is complete.

Error is
highlighted here

Spelling and Grammar: English (U.K.)	? X
Not in Dictionary:	
We also want you to begin to get an **insightr** into how powerful coaching is and the level of improvement you can expect when you coach your people.	**Ignore** — Ignore error
	Ignore All — Ignore all instances of this error
	Add — Add word to dictionary
Suggestions:	
insight	**Change**
insights	**Change All**
	AutoCorrect
☑ Check grammar	
?	**Options...** / Undo / **Cancel**

Set spelling and grammar options

1 In the **Tools** menu, select **Options**.

2 Click on the **Spelling & Grammar** tab.

3 Select appropriate spelling and grammar options.

4 Click **OK**.

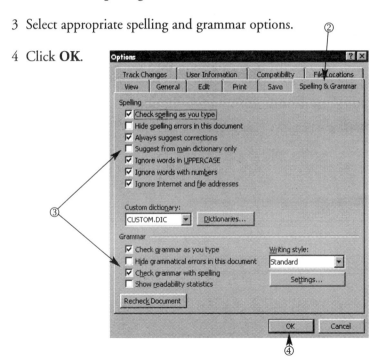

Use AutoCorrect

As its name implies, the AutoCorrect feature automatically corrects common keyboard typos and spelling mistakes as you type.

1 In the **Tools** menu, select **AutoCorrect**.

2 The complete list of correction rules is displayed in the drop-down list.

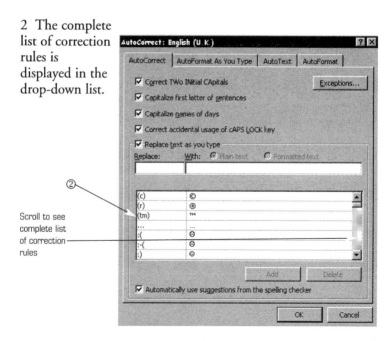

②

Scroll to see complete list of correction rules

Add an AutoCorrect entry

1 In the **Tools** menu, select **AutoCorrect**.

2 Type the symbol or misspelled word in the left-hand column.

3 Type the replacement symbol or text in the right-hand column.

4 Click **Add**.

5 Click **OK**.

Delete an AutoCorrect entry

1 In the **Tools** menu, select **AutoCorrect**.

2 Locate the AutoCorrect entry that you want to delete from the drop-down list.

3 Click **Delete**.

4 Click **OK**.

Use the thesaurus

1 Right-click on the word that you want to replace.

2 In the **Synonyms** menu, select an alternative word.

OR

Select **Thesaurus**.

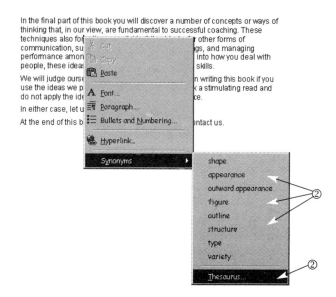

3 Select one of the meanings listed.

4 Select a suitable synonym.

5 Click **Replace**.

tip

To see more word choices, highlight a synonym and click Look Up.

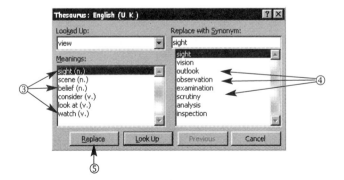

Create AutoText entry

If you often find yourself typing the same words and phrases, you can store them as AutoText entries in Word. The next time you start to type the word or phrase, Word will complete it for you.

1 Enter the word or phrase into a document.

2 Highlight it.

3 In the **Insert** menu, point to **AutoText** and select **New**.

4 Word will suggest a name for the AutoText entry, or you can add a name of your own.

5 Click **OK**.

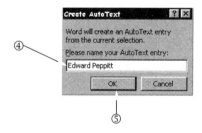

Use an AutoText entry

1 In your document, start to type the AutoText name.

2 As you type, the AutoComplete tip box appears with the full AutoText name.

3 Press **[Enter]**.

tip

If the AutoComplete tip box does not appear, you may find that this feature is switched off. In the Insert menu, point to AutoText, and select AutoText. Select the **Show AutoComplete tip for AutoText and dates** check box.

Switch off proofing for a specific section of text

1 Highlight the text that you do not want to be proofed.

2 In the **Tools** menu, point to **Language** and select **Set Language**.

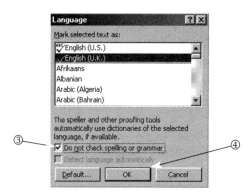

3 Click to select **Do not check spelling or grammar**.

4 Click **OK**.

Create a new dictionary

You may wish to store technical terms, as well as other specific words or phrases that you use, in your own custom dictionary.

1 In the **Tools** menu, select **Options**.

2 Click to select the **Spelling & Grammar** tab.

3 Click **Dictionaries**.

4 Click **New**.

5 Give the new dictionary a name and click **Save**.

6 Select an appropriate language.

7 Click **OK**.

8 Select the custom dictionary that you want to add new words to.

9 Click **OK**.

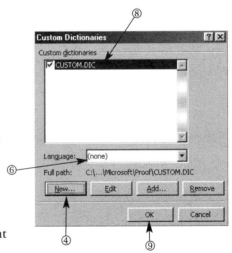

Bullets and Numbering

Convert text to a bulleted or numbered list

1 Highlight the text that you want to be bulleted or numbered.

2 Click on the appropriate icon in the formatting toolbar.

Numbers   Bullets

Convert bullets to numbers

1 Highlight the bulleted list.

2 Click on the **Numbers** icon shown above.

Create a bulleted or numbered list as you type

1 Move cursor to the point where you want a bulleted or numbered list.

2 Click on the appropriate icon in the formatting toolbar.

3 Begin typing.

4 Create the next bulleted or numbered point by pressing **[Enter]**.

Add items to a bulleted or numbered list

1 Click at the end of the last line of the list.

2 Press **[Enter]**.

3 A new bullet or numbered point will appear automatically.

Customize bullets and numbers

1 Highlight the numbered or bulleted list.

2 In the **Format** menu, select **Bullets and Numbering**.

3 Select an appropriate number or bullet style.

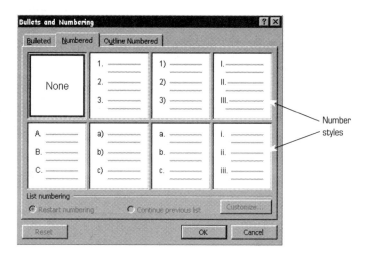

Number styles

4 Click **Customize...** for further options.

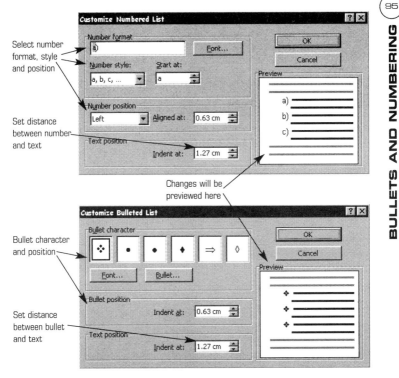

Select number format, style and position

Set distance between number and text

Changes will be previewed here

Bullet character and position

Set distance between bullet and text

5 Click **OK** when finished.

Undo a bulleted or numbered list

BULLETS AND NUMBERING

1 Highlight the bulleted or numbered list.

2 Click on the appropriate icon in the formatting toolbar.

OR

1 Highlight the bulleted or numbered list.

2 In the **Format** menu, select **Bullets and Numbering**.

3 Select **None**.

4 Click **OK**.

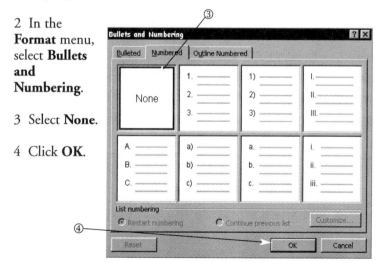

Create an outline numbered list

You can create an outline numbered list with up to nine levels.

1 In the **Format** menu, select **Bullets and Numbering**.

2 Click on the **Outline Numbered** tab.

3 Click to select an appropriate outline numbering format.

4 Click **OK**.

5 Type your numbered list.

To demote a list item to a lower numbering level, click .

To promote a list item to a higher numbering level, click .

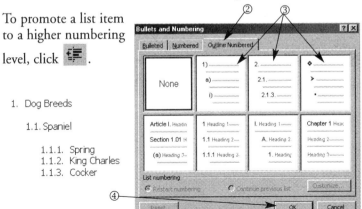

Columns

Put text into columns

1 Highlight the text that you want to put into columns.

2 Click ![icon].

3 Drag mouse across number of columns that you want.

4 Click on mouse.

Drag mouse
across
columns

Revert to a single column

1 Highlight the text in columns.

2 Click ![icon].

3 Drag mouse across to single column.

4 Click on mouse.

Alter the column layout

1 Click in any part of the document with columns.

2 In the **Format** menu, select **Columns**.

3 Change the number, width and spacing of columns.

4 Click **OK**.

Number of columns

Width of spacing of coumns

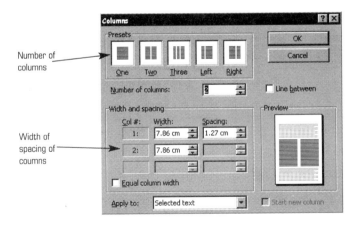

Tables

Create a simple table

1 Move the cursor to the point in your document where you want a table.

2 In the **Table** menu, select **Insert**, then **Table**.

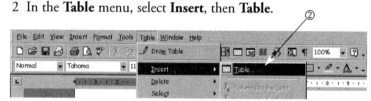

3 Enter the appropriate number of columns and rows that you need.

4 Click **OK**.

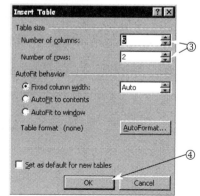

Convert text to a table

1 Insert separator characters (e.g. commas) into text to indicate where columns should be placed.

2 Highlight the text that you want to convert.

3 In the **Table** menu, point to **Convert** and select **Text to Table**.

4 Select the appropriate separator character where indicated.

5 Click **OK**.

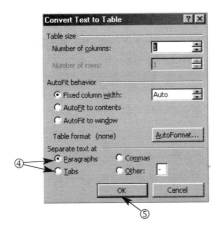

Draw a table

1 In the **Table** menu, select **Draw Table**.

  OR

  Click ⊞ on the formatting toolbar.

2 Click on ✏.

3 Click and drag the pencil icon across the page until table outline is the right size, and release the mouse.

4 Add columns and rows inside the table outline using the same drawing tool. Draw vertical lines to create columns, and horizontal lines to create rows.

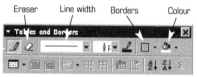

Eraser   Line width   Borders   Colour

Draw table

tip

You can undo the most recent row or column you have added by clicking on ↶ . You can undo any other part of the table by selecting ✐ and dragging it over the lines to remove.

Select a complete table

Click on ⊞ in the top left-hand corner of the table.

OR

In the **Table** menu, click **Select** and then **Table**.

Charlotte	Tim

Select a row

1 Move the cursor to the left of the table until it changes to a white arrow pointing to the row that you wish to select.

2 Click once.

OR

1 Click inside the first cell in the row you wish to select.

2 Drag the mouse across all the cells in that row.

Select a column

1 Move the cursor to above the table until it changes to a black arrow pointing down to the column you wish to select.

2 Click once.

OR

1 Click inside the first cell in the column you wish to select.

2 Drag the mouse down all the cells in that column.

Sort a column within a table

1 Highlight the column or cells that you want to sort.

2 In the **Table** menu, select **Sort**.

3 Select appropriate sort options.

4 Click **Options**.

5 Select **Sort column only**.

6 Click **OK**.

7 Click **OK**.

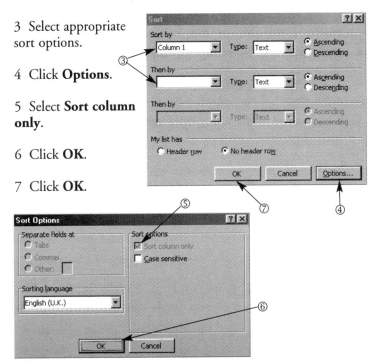

Use Table AutoFormat

1 Click anywhere inside the table.

2 In the **Table** menu, select **Table AutoFormat**.

3 Choose an appropriate table format.

4 Select other formatting options.

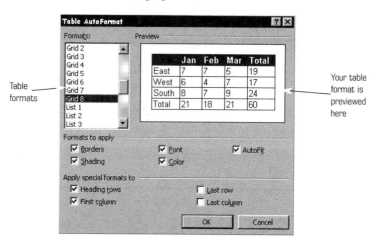

Table formats

Your table format is previewed here

5 Click **OK**.

Add rows to a table

1 Highlight the row above or below where you wish to add a new row.

2 In the **Table** menu, select **Insert** and then either **Rows Above** or **Rows Below**.

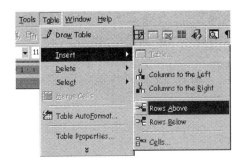

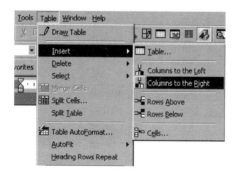
Add columns to a table

1 Highlight the column next to where you wish to add a new column.

2 In the **Table** menu, select **Insert** and then either **Columns to the left** or **Columns to the right**.

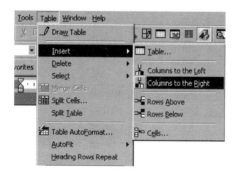

Insert a tab inside a cell

If you press **[Tab]** inside a table, the cursor moves automatically to the next cell. Sometimes, however, you need to place a tab within a cell.

1 Click in table cell.

2 Hold down **[Ctrl]** and press **[Tab]**.

Add up figures in a table column

If your table contains figures and other data, you can perform simple calculations without the need to incorporate an Excel spreadsheet.

1 Select the table containing figures that you want to add up.

2 In the **View** menu, point to **Toolbars** and select **Tables and Borders**.

3 Click inside the empty cell at the end of the column of figures.

4 Click the **AutoSum** button.

Add up figures in a table row

1 Select the table containing figures that you want to add up.

2 In the **View** menu, point to **Toolbars** and select **Tables and Borders**.

3 Click inside the empty cell at the end of the row of figures.

4 Click the **AutoSum** button.

Update calculations in a table

If you make changes to the figures in a table, the totals will not recalculate automatically like in Excel.

1 Select the table.

2 Press **[F9]**.

Display Picture toolbar

The Picture toolbar contains all the tools you are likely to need to insert and edit pictures and simple graphics.

In the **View** menu, point to **Toolbars** and select **Picture**.

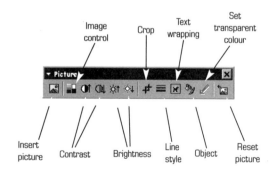

Image control   Crop   Text wrapping   Set transparent colour

Insert picture   Contrast   Brightness   Line style   Object   Reset picture

Display Drawing toolbar

The Drawing toolbar contains all the tools you are likely to need
to draw and amend common shapes and lines.

In the **View** menu, point to **Toolbars** and select **Drawing**.

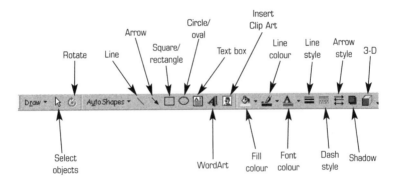

Insert a picture into a document

1 Move cursor to where you want to insert the picture.

2 In the **Insert** menu, point to **Picture** and select **From File**.

3 Navigate to the drive or directory where the picture file is located.

4 Select the picture file.

5 Click **Insert**.

Edit a picture within your document

1 Click on the picture/graphic to select it. A frame with eight black sizing handles will appear around the picture.

2 Click and drag one of the black sizing handles to resize the picture.

3 Right-click and select **Format Picture** to make changes to other properties of the picture.

tip

To maintain the picture's proportion, click and drag on a corner sizing handle.

Insert Clip Art

1 Move cursor to where you want to insert Clip Art in your document.

2 In the **Insert** menu, point to **Picture** and select **Clip Art**.

3 Click on the **Pictures** tab.

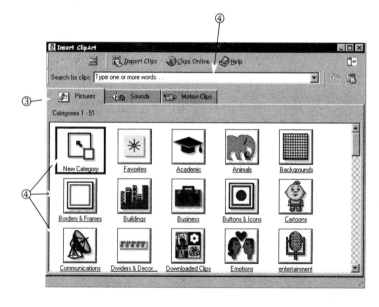

4 Select a category **OR** Enter a keyword for what you are looking for, and press **[Enter]**.

5 Select a picture.

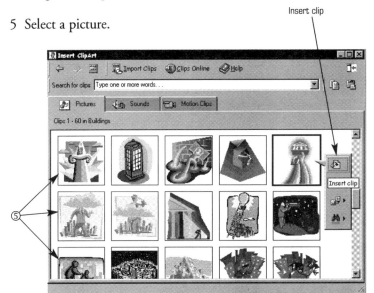

6 Preview the picture if desired.

7 Click **Insert Clip**.

8 Close Insert Clip Art dialog box.

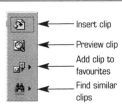

Insert clip

Preview clip

Add clip to favourites

Find similar clips

Crop a picture with mouse

1 Click on picture to select it.

2 In the **View** menu, point to **Toolbars** and select **Picture**.

3 Click  on Picture toolbar.

4 Move mouse pointer over a sizing handle.

5 Click and drag sizing handle towards the centre of the picture/graphic.

6 Repeat for the other sizing handles as required.

7 Click away from the picture to deselect it.

Crop/resize a picture using menu

1 Double-click on picture to open Format Picture dialog box.

   OR

   Right-click on picture and select **Format Picture**.

2 Click on **Picture** tab.

3 Enter crop values.

4 Click on **Size** tab.

5 Enter size values.

6 Click **OK**.

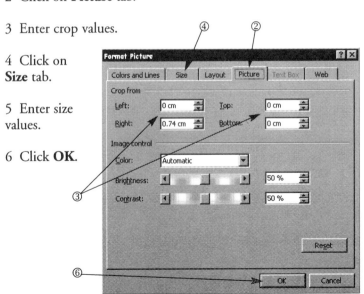

Resize a picture

1 Click picture to select it.

2 Move mouse pointer to a sizing handle.

3 Click and drag the sizing handle until image is the desired size.

tip

To keep the resized image in proportion, click and drag a corner sizing handle only.

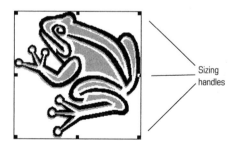

Sizing
handles

Adjust contrast/brightness of picture

1 Click picture to select it.

2 In the **View** menu, point to **Toolbars** and select **Picture**.

3 Click on appropriate button on Picture toolbar.

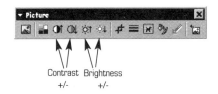

Contrast Brightness
+/-   +/-

tip

You may find that a colour Clip Art file prints better on a black and white printer if you adjust the contrast and brightness first.

Wrap text around a picture

1 Display the Picture toolbar.

2 Click picture to select it.

3 Click text wrapping button on Picture toolbar.

4 Choose text wrapping option from drop-down menu.

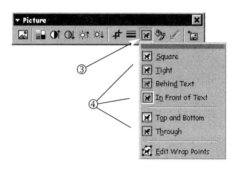

Keep picture in line with text

1 Click picture to select it.

2 In the **Format** menu, select **Picture**.

3 Click on **Layout** tab.

4 Click **In line with text**.

5 Click **OK**.

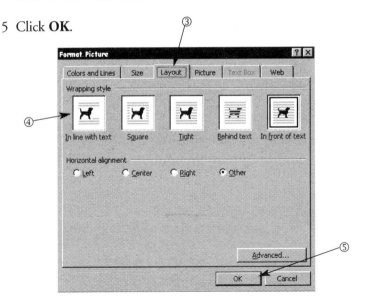

Copy a picture

GRAPHICS

1 Click picture to select it.

2 Click .

3 Move cursor to where you want to copy the picture to.

4 Click ▓.

Move a picture

1 Click picture to select it.

2 Click and drag to new location.

3 Release mouse.

tip

If you have chosen to keep the picture in line with text, you will only be able to move it to the start of a new line. If you have chosen a different text wrapping option, you will be able to move the picture to any point in your document.

Group drawing objects

1 Hold down **[Shift]** and select the objects that you want to group together.

2 On the Drawing toolbar, click **Draw** and select **Group**.

Ungroup drawing objects

1 Click to select the group.

2 On the Drawing toolbar, click **Draw** and select **Ungroup**.

Fix the position of a picture

1 Right-click on the picture and select **Format Picture**.

2 Click on the **Layout** tab.

3 Click on the **Advanced** tab.

4 Click on the **Picture Position** tab.

5 Enter values for the vertical and horizontal anchors.

6 Click **OK**.

You can fix a picture to a paragraph so that the two move together. Select the 'Move object with text' check box to ensure that the picture moves up or down with the paragraph it's anchored to. Select the 'Lock anchor' check box to ensure that the picture remains anchored to the same paragraph when you move it.

Insert AutoShapes

1 Display the Drawing toolbar.

2 Click **AutoShapes** on Drawing toolbar to see the common shapes you can draw automatically.

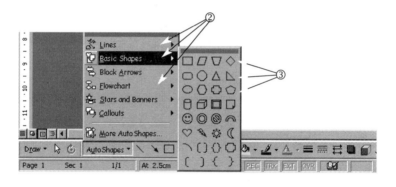

3 Click on an AutoShape to select it.

4 Click and drag mouse to create the shape in your document.

5 Release mouse.

6 Click shape to select it, and format it using tools on the
Drawing toolbar.

To keep the dimensions of the shape in proportion, hold down
[Shift] while clicking and dragging the mouse.

Draw/edit lines

1 Display Drawing toolbar.

2 Click  to select it.

3 Move mouse pointer to where you want to draw a line.

4 Click and drag mouse to draw line.

5 Release mouse.

6 Click on one of the sizing handles to resize the line.

7 Click and drag
line to move it.

8 Right-click on
line and select
Format AutoShape.

9 Amend line weight and style, colour and size.

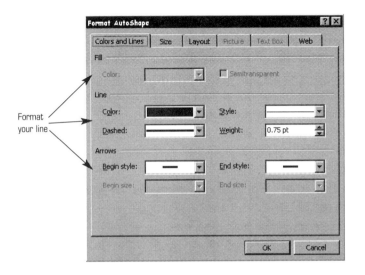

Format your line

10 Click **OK** when finished.

Draw simple ovals and rectangles

GRAPHICS

1 Display Drawing toolbar.

2 Click on □ or ○.

3 Move mouse pointer to where you want to draw your shape.

4 Click and drag mouse to draw shape.

5 If you want to draw either a circle or a square, hold down **[Shift]** while clicking and dragging.

Add a caption to a picture

1 Click to select the picture or graphic.

2 In the **Insert** menu, select **Caption**.

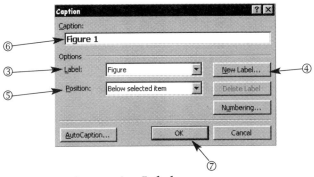

3 Select an appropriate caption **Label**.

4 You can add a new caption label by clicking on **New Label**.

5 Select a position for the caption from the drop-down menu.

6 Enter the caption text.

7 Click **OK**.

Add captions automatically

1 In the **Insert** menu, select **Caption**.

2 Click on **AutoCaption**.

3 Click to turn on automatic captions for any item in the list.

4 Select an appropriate caption **Label**.

5 You can add a new caption label by clicking on **New Label**.

6 Select a position for the caption from the drop-down menu.

7 Repeat steps 3–6 to add automatic captions for other items in the list.

8 Click **OK**.

Figure 1

Other Documents

Insert a new Excel worksheet into a document

1 Move the cursor to the point in your document where you want to insert a worksheet.

2 Click 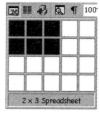 .

3 Click and drag to select the number of rows and columns to be included.

4 Worksheet will be inserted.

5 Click outside worksheet to close it and return to the main document.

Click and drag to select rows and columns

Edit Excel worksheet

1 Double-click on worksheet to open it.

2 Amend/edit as required using Excel tools on menu bar.

3 Click outside worksheet area to close it and return to main document.

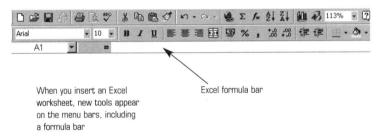

When you insert an Excel
worksheet, new tools appear
on the menu bars, including
a formula bar

Excel formula bar

Borders and Shading

Add a page border

1 In the **Format** menu, select **Borders and Shading**.

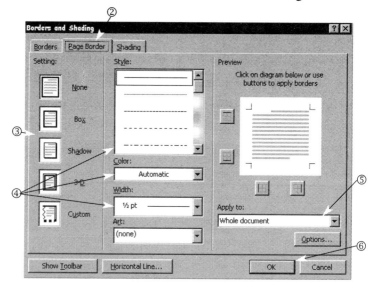

2 Click on **Page Border** tab.

3 Choose a page border setting.

4 Choose a style, colour and width for your page border.

5 Select the part of your document that you want to display the page border.

6 Click **OK**.

7 Click **Options** for further customization.

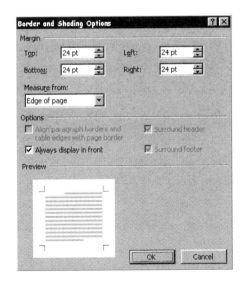

Add an art border

1 In the **Format** menu, select **Borders and Shading**.

2 Click on **Page Border** tab.

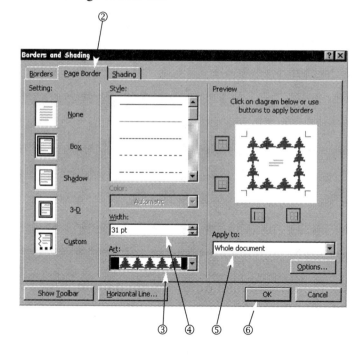

3 Choose an art border from the drop-down menu.

4 Select the width of your art border.

5 Select the part of your document that you want to display the art border.

6 Click **OK**.

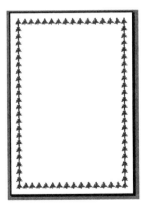

Place a border around text

1 Highlight the text that you want to place a border around.

2 In the **Format** menu, select **Borders and Shading**.

3 Select border style, colour and width.

4 Click **OK**.

To apply a quick border, click on downward-pointing arrow to the right of 🔲 ▼ , and select the border you want to apply.

Place a border around a paragraph

1 Click anywhere inside paragraph.

2 Click on downward-pointing arrow to the right of .

3 Select the border that you want to apply.

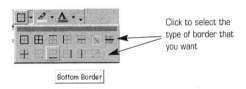

Click to select the
type of border that
you want

Bottom Border

Create a custom border

1 Select the text/paragraph around which you want to add the border.

2 In the **Format** menu, select **Borders and Shading**.

3 Click on **Borders** tab.

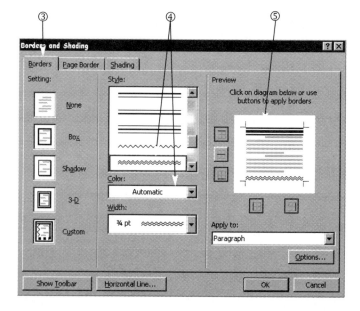

4 Select appropriate style and colour.

5 In the Preview screen, click individual borders to remove them or re-apply them.

You can specify a different style, width and colour for each border line.

Place a border around an object

1 Right-click on the object and select **Borders and Shading**.

2 Click on **Borders** tab.

3 Select the border that you want to use.

4 Click **OK**.

Apply shading to text

1 Highlight the text that you want to shade.

2 In the **Format** menu, select **Borders and Shading**.

3 Click **Shading** tab.

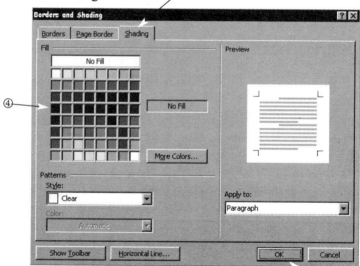

4 Select the shading colour that you want to use.

5 Click **OK**.

tip

You can display a Tables and Borders toolbar so that you can add tables, borders and shading more quickly. In the View menu, point to Toolbars and select Tables and Borders.

Add a line underneath a paragraph

Sometimes you may want to add a line underneath a paragraph for emphasis.

1 Click on last line of paragraph.

2 Click on downward-pointing arrow to the right of .

3 Select ▣.

Change borders

1 Highlight the text/paragraph that contains the border.

2 In the **Format** menu, select **Borders and Shading**.

3 Click on **Borders** tab.

4 Amend width, style and colour of border.

5 Click **OK**.

Remove borders

1 Highlight the text/paragraph that contains the border.

2 Click on downward-pointing arrow to the right of ⬜▾.

3 Click ▨.

OR

1 Highlight the text/paragraph that contains the border.

2 In the **Format** menu, select **Borders and Shading**.

3 Click **None**.

4 Click **OK**.

Charts

Create a simple chart

Word comes with Microsoft Chart to make drawing a chart really straightforward.

1 In the **Insert** menu, point to **Picture** and select **Chart**.

2 Replace the sample data and headings in the datasheet with your own.

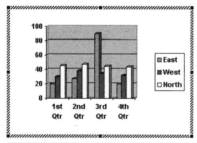

		A	B	C	D	E
		1st Qtr	2nd Qtr	3rd Qtr	4th Qtr	
1	East	20.4	27.4	90	20.4	
2	West	30.6	38.6	34.6	31.6	
3	North	45.9	46.9	45	43.9	
4						

3 Use the toolbar provided to amend the format of any chart element.

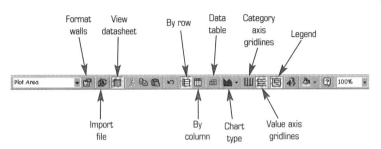

4 Click outside the chart to return to the main document.

Edit a chart

1 Double-click on chart to open it.

2 Amend/edit chart data or chart appearance as required.

3 Click outside the chart to return to the main document.

Insert an Excel chart

1 Open Excel worksheet and use Chart Wizard to create the chart.

2 Save workbook.

3 Select and copy the chart.

4 Open Word document.

5 Move cursor to where you want the chart to appear.

6 Click .

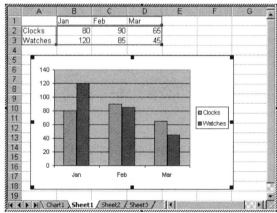

Edit an Excel chart

1 Double-click on chart.

2 Use the Excel toolbar to edit the chart.

3 Click on worksheet containing data.

4 Edit data as required.

5 Click back to chart tab in workbook.

6 Click

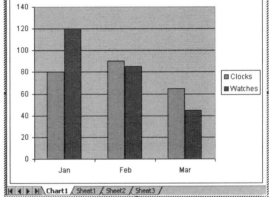

outside chart to return to main document.

To add a caption or label to a chart, see *Add a caption to a picture* on page 133.

Mail Merges

If you want to send the same letter to a number of people, Word's mail merge facility allows you to automate many stages of the process.

You need two items to perform a mail merge:

- Main document (e.g. the letter that you want to send).

- Data source (e.g. the names and addresses of recipients).

Create a letter or document to merge

1 Start a new document, and write the letter that you want to send. Do not type in any names or addresses at this stage.

2 In the **Tools** menu, select **Mail Merge**.

3 Under the **Main Document** heading, click **Create** and select **Form Letters**.

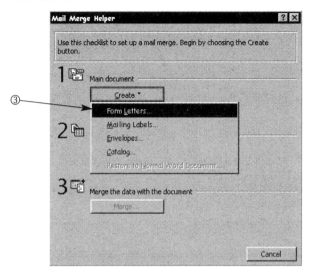

4 Click **Active Window** when prompted.

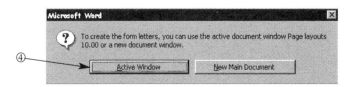

Create a data source

If you do not already have a file containing the names and addresses you need for the mail merge, you need to create one now.

1 Open the letter or document that you want to merge.

2 In the **Tools** menu, select **Mail Merge**.

3 Under the **Data Source** heading, click **Get Data** and select **Create Data Source**.

4 Add or remove field names until you have all the field names you require to enter the data.

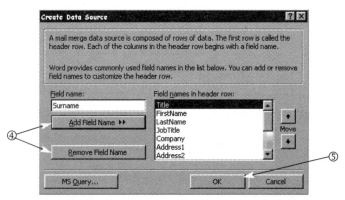

5 Click **OK**.

6 Save your data source onto your hard disk.

7 Click **Edit Data Source**.

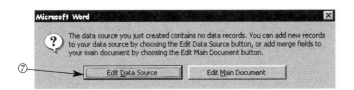

8 Enter the data (names and addresses) one at a time. Click **Add New** to enter each new name and address.

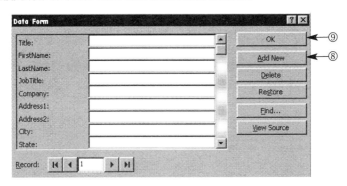

9 Click **OK** when complete.

Open data source

Word can collect data for your mail merge from a table created in Word, an Excel spreadsheet or an Access database (as well as a number of other common file formats).

1 Open the letter or document that you want to merge.

2 In the **Tools** menu, select **Mail Merge**.

3 Under the **Data Source** heading, click **Get Data** and select **Open Data Source**.

4 Navigate to the file you wish to extract data from.

5 Click **OK**.

Use an Excel spreadsheet as a data source

1 In the **Mail Merge** menu, click **Get Data** and select **Open Data Source**.

2 Select **MS Excel Worksheets** where indicated.

3 Navigate to your spreadsheet and double-click to open it.

4 Select either a single worksheet or the entire spreadsheet.

5 Click **OK**.

Use an Access database as a data
source

1 In the **Mail Merge** menu, click **Get Data** and select **Open
Data Source**.

2 Select **MS Access Databases** where indicated.

3 Navigate to your database and double-click to open it.

4 Select the table or query containing the data you need.

5 Click **OK**.

Edit data source

You may want to add, remove or edit data in a data source before merging the data with your letter.

1 In the **Tools** menu, select **Mail Merge**.

2 Under the **Data Source** heading, click **Edit** and select the data file.

3 Make any changes to the data.

4 Click **OK**.

Specify where merged data will appear in document

1 Open the letter that you wish to merge.

2 Move cursor to where you want to add the names, addresses or any other data.

3 Click on **Insert Merge Field** and select the appropriate data field.

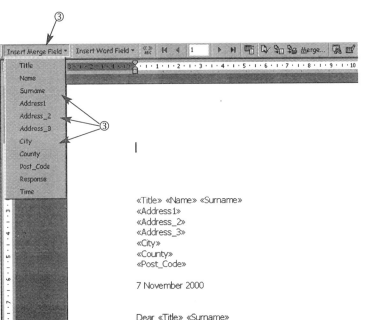

4 Repeat until your letter includes all data fields that you want to merge.

1 Open the letter that you wish to merge.

2 Click Merge... on Mail Merge toolbar.

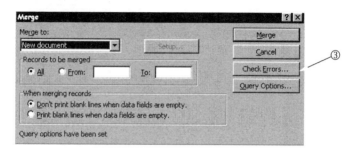

3 Click **Check errors**.

4 Select appropriate option.

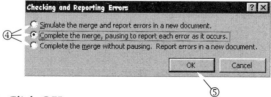

5 Click **OK**.

Perform the mail merge

1 Click **Merge...** on Mail Merge toolbar.

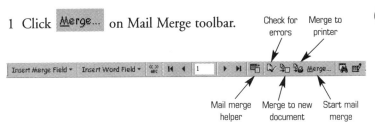

2 Specify whether to merge to new document, direct to the printer or to an e-mail.

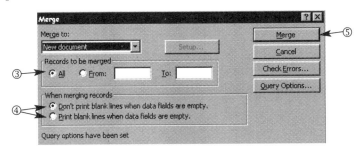

3 Specify which records to merge.

4 Specify what to do with blank records.

5 Click **Merge**.

View the mail merge before printing

Before you go ahead and print the merged document, you may wish to view how the letters look on the screen.

1 Click 《》 ABC on Mail Merge toolbar.

2 Click ▶ to view each merged letter in turn.

3 If you spot any errors in the actual letter, correct them in the original document.

4 If you spot any errors in the names and addresses, correct them in the data source file.

5 When you are satisfied with how the letters look on the screen, perform the mail merge.

Filter/sort data source

You may only wish to send your letter to certain names in the data source.

1 In the Mail Merge menu, click **Query Options**.

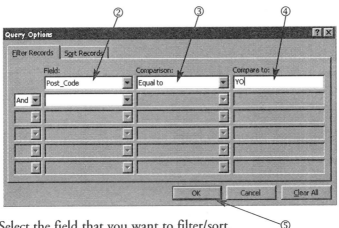

2 Select the field that you want to filter/sort.

3 Select appropriate comparison type.

4 Type filter criteria in **Compare to** field.

5 Click **OK**.

Merge address labels

1 Open and save a new document.

2 In the **Tools** menu, select **Mail Merge**.

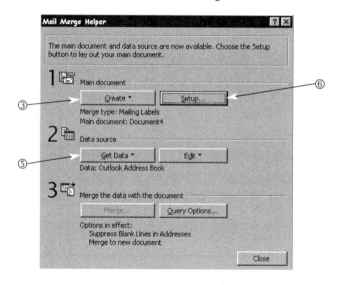

3 Under the **Main Document** heading, click **Create** and select
Mailing Labels.

4 Click **Active Window**.

5 Under the **Data Source** heading, click **Get Data** and choose your data source.

6 Under the **Main Document** heading, click **Setup**.

7 Select mailing label type and printer information.

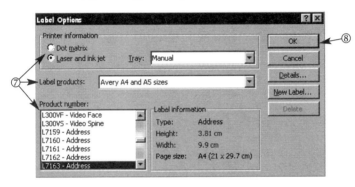

8 Click **OK**.

Create merged address labels

1 Click **Insert Merge Field** and select each data field you wish
to include in turn.

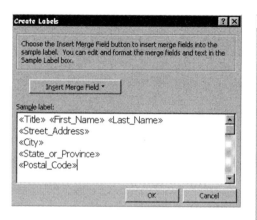

2 Add any spaces, punctuation or new lines as required.

3 Click **OK** when complete.

4 Click **Close** in **Mail Merge** menu.

```
«Title» «First_Name» «Last_Name»        «Title» «First_Name» «Last_Name»
«Street_Address»                         «Street_Address»
«City»                                   «City»
«State_or_Province»                      «State_or_Province»
«Postal_Code»                            «Postal_Code»


«Title» «First_Name» «Last_Name»        «Title» «First_Name» «Last_Name»
«Street_Address»                         «Street_Address»
«City»                                   «City»
«State_or_Province»                      «State_or_Province»
«Postal_Code»                            «Postal_Code»
```

5 Click 🔲 to merge to new document.

6 Click 🔳 to merge straight to the printer.

7 Click Merge... for other merge options.

Editing

Undo mistakes

1 Click 🖙 to undo the most recent action you have performed.

2 Keep clicking 🖙 to undo preceding actions one at a time.

3 Click the downward-pointing arrow to the right of 🖙 to view a complete list of actions that you can undo.

Restore an action you have undone

1 Click 🖙.

2 Keep clicking 🖙 to restore actions one at a time.

3 Click downward-pointing arrow to the right of 🖙 to view a complete list of actions that you can redo.

Replace words in a document

1 In the **Edit** menu, select **Replace**.

2 Click on the **Replace** tab.

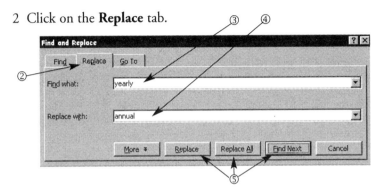

3 Type the text to be replaced into the **Find what** field.

4 Type the replacement text into the **Replace with** field.

5 Click on one of the
replacement options at the
bottom of the dialog box.

6 Click **OK** or **Close** when
replacement operation is
complete.

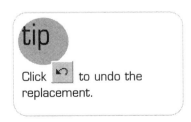

tip

Click ⟳ to undo the
replacement.

Find text within a document

In a large document, you can quickly lose a word, sentence or paragraph. The Find function will help you to locate it.

1 In the **Edit** menu, select **Find**.

2 Click on the **Find** tab.

3 Enter some/all of the text you are looking for.

4 Click **Find next**.

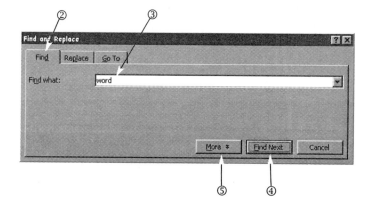

5 Click **More** to broaden or narrow search criteria.

tip

You can search in part of a document only. Highlight the part of the text that you want to search in before following steps 1–5.

Go to a specific item

1 In the **Edit** menu, select **Go To**.

2 Select the type of object that you want to go to.

EITHER

3 Enter a page or other object number.

4 Click **Go To**.

OR

3 Leave object number blank.

4 Click **Next** or **Previous**.

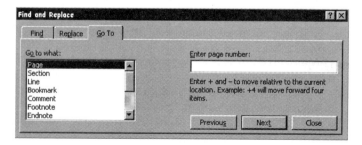

Add a page break

1 Move cursor to the point in the text where you want to insert a page break.

2 In the **Insert** menu, select **Break**.

3 Select **Page break**.

4 Click **OK**.

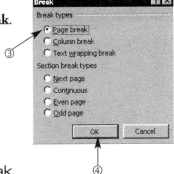

Remove a page break

1 Click ¶ to show paragraph marks.

2 Highlight the dotted page break line.

3 Press the **[Delete]** key.

Add a section break

1 Move cursor to the point in the text where you want to insert a page break.

2 In the **Insert** menu, select **Break**.

3 Select appropriate section break type.

4 Click **OK**.

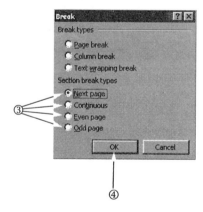

Remove a section break

1 Click ▐¶ to show paragraph marks.

2 Highlight the dotted section break line.

3 Press the **[Delete]** key.

Change the type of section break

1 Click inside the section that you want to change.

2 In the **File** menu, select **Page Setup**.

3 Click on the **Layout** tab.

4 Select the desired **Section start** type.

5 Click **OK**.

Apply line numbering

1 In the **File** menu, select **Page Setup**.

2 Click on **Layout** tab.

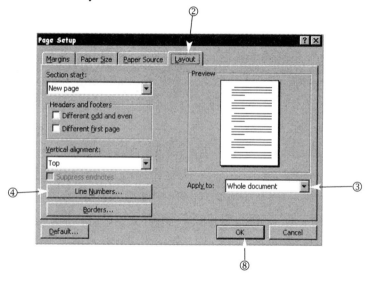

3 In the **Apply to** drop-down menu, select **Whole document**.

4 Click **Line Numbers**.

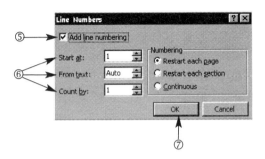

5 Click **Add line numbering**.

6 Specify any other options required.

7 Click **OK**.

8 Click **OK**.

Create a table of contents

In order to create a table of contents automatically, it is essential that you have used Styles (e.g. Heading 1, Heading 2) within your document. See page 212.

1 Move cursor to the point in your document where you want your table of contents to appear.

2 In the **Insert** menu, select **Index and Tables**.

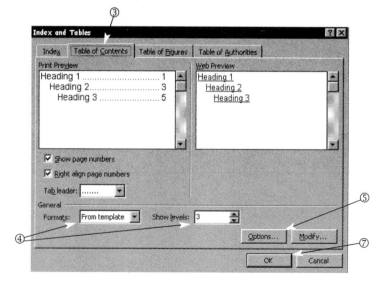

3 Click on **Table of Contents** tab.

4 Choose a suitable format.

5 Select any other options required.

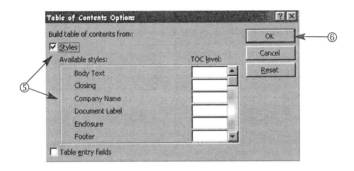

6 Click **OK**.

7 Click **OK**.

Update a table of contents

1 Edit the document that has a table of contents and save the changes you have made.

2 Move mouse pointer to the left of the first line of the table of contents.

3 Click to select the table of contents.

4 Right-click on the table of contents, and select **Update**.

5 Make an appropriate selection.

6 Click **OK**.

Create an index

First you must mark the entries for your index within your document.

1 In the **Insert** menu, select **Index and Tables**.

2 Click on the **Index** tab.

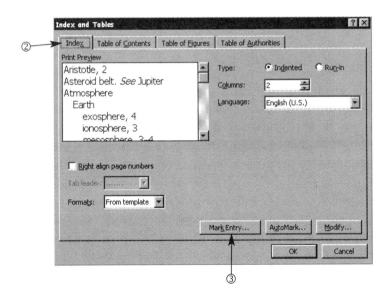

3 Click **Mark Index Entry**.

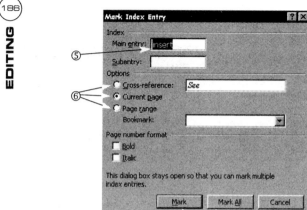

4 Highlight the first item you want to insert into the index.

5 Click in the **Main entry** field to insert the highlighted word into the dialog box.

6 Select from one of the **Options**.

7 Click **Mark** (or **Mark All** if you want to insert all occurrences of this word/phrase in the index).

Add a page range to an index

1 Select the text within the page range to be included.

2 In the **Insert** menu, select **Bookmark**.

3 Enter a name for the bookmark and click **Add**.

4 In the **Mark Index Entry** dialog box, type in the **Main entry**.

5 Select **Page range**.

6 Select the bookmark name.

7 Click **Mark**.

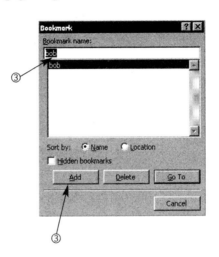

Compile the index

1 Close the **Mark Index Entry** dialog box (if you have not done so already).

2 Move cursor to the end of the document.

3 In the **Insert** menu, select **Index and Tables**.

4 Click on the **Index** tab.

5 Select an index type and style.

6 Click **OK**.

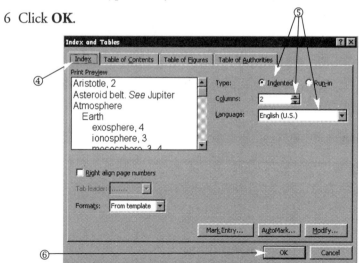

Track user changes

You may wish to track the changes that have been made to a document.

1 Open the document that you want to track.

2 In the **View** menu, point to **Toolbars** and select **Reviewing**.

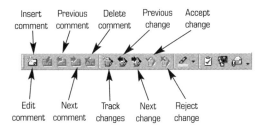

Insert comment   Previous comment   Delete comment   Previous change   Accept change

Edit comment   Next comment   Track changes   Next change   Reject change

3 Click to start reviewing changes.

4 Changes made will be highlighted.

Multiple Documents

Open multiple documents

Word allows you to open and work on several documents at the same time. With one or more documents already open:

1 In the **File** menu, select **Open**.

2 Navigate to the next document that you want to work on.

3 Click **Open**.

A new window appears containing this document.

You can start a new document while continuing to work on another.

- In the **File** menu, select **New**.

  OR

- Click on .

Open multiple documents at the same time

You may wish to work on several related documents at the same time.

1 In the **File** menu, select **Open**.

2 Navigate to the first document that you want to open.

3 Hold down **[Ctrl]**.

4 Navigate to the next document.

5 Repeat until you have highlighted all the documents that you want to open.

6 Click **Open**.

Switch between open documents

In the **Window** menu, select the document that you want to work on.

This document now becomes active. The other open documents are still available but remain inactive until you select them using the method described above.

You can also switch between documents by clicking on one of the files listed on the taskbar at the bottom of the screen.

Cut/copy text between documents

Word allows you to cut, copy and paste between a number of open documents.

1 Open the document that you want to cut or copy text from.

2 Click or ▣ as required.

3 Open the document in which you want to paste the text.

4 Move cursor to desired place in the document.

5 Click ▣ .

View several documents at once

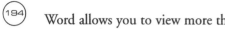

MULTIPLE DOCUMENTS

(194)

Word allows you to view more than one document on your screen at the same time.

1 Open the documents that you would like to view together.

2 In the **Window** menu, select **Arrange All**.

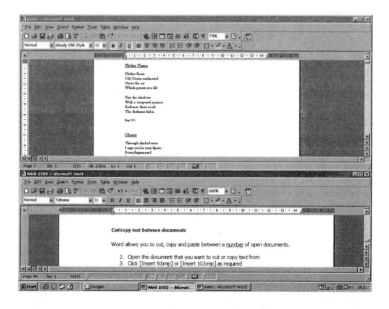

tip

With several documents open and visible at the same time, only one will be active. This is the one with the shaded menu bar.

Split the document window

You may wish to display two parts of the same document simultaneously.

1 In the **Window** menu, select **Split**.

2 Drag the shaded line into the desired position, then click once to fix it.

You can now scroll to different parts of the same document in each of the visible panes.

Templates

Create a new template

1 In the **File** menu, select **New**.

2 Click on **Template**.

3 Select **Blank Document**.

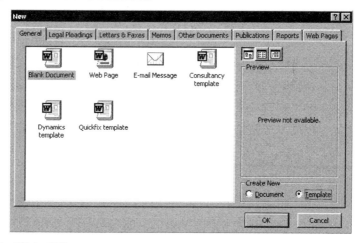

4 Click **OK**.

5 Enter text and features that will be common to all documents based on the new template.

6 Format text and layout as you want it to appear.

7 In the **File** menu, select **Save As**.

8 Choose a suitable name for your template.

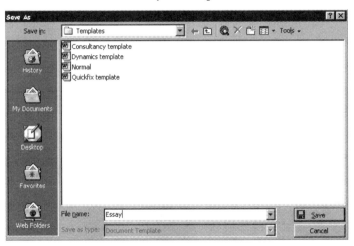

9 Click **OK**.

Now you will be able to select this template whenever you select **New** in the **File** menu.

Modify an existing template

1 In the **File** menu, select **Open**.

2 In the drop-down menu, select **Document Templates**.

3 Navigate to template and select it.

4 Click **Open**.

5 Make any changes/modifications.

6 In the **File** menu, select **Save As** to save the modified template under a new name.

OR

In the **File** menu, select **Save** to save the modified template under its original name.

Usually templates are stored in the Windows directory, in a folder called Application Data.

Convert a document into a template

1 Open the document you want to use as a template.

2 In the **File** menu, select **Save As**.

3 In the **Save as type** drop-down menu, select **Document template**.

4 Name your new template.

5 Click **Save**.

Use a template

1 Click **Start** and select **New Office Document**.

2 Navigate to the template that you want to use.

3 Click to select template.

4 Click **OK**.

Text Boxes

Create a text box

1 In the **View** menu, point to **Toolbars** and select **Drawing**.

2 Click on [icon].

3 Click and drag mouse to draw text box.

4 Release mouse.

5 Click inside text box and start typing.

Format a text box

1 Click on text box frame to select it.

2 Right-click and select **Format Text Box**.

3 You can format the size, colour and position of the text box.

4 Click **OK**.

You can align the text inside a text box. Click inside the text box and select one of the text alignment icons.

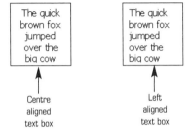

Centre aligned text box

Left aligned text box

tip

You can also resize the text box. Click on the text box frame, and use the sizing handles that appear around the frame.

Create a text box link

You can flow text between two or more text boxes.

1 Click on frame of the first text box.

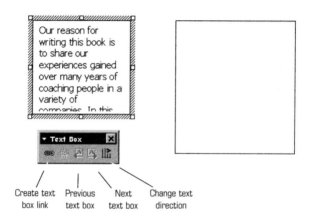

Our reason for writing this book is to share our experiences gained over many years of coaching people in a variety of companies. In this

▾ Text Box ✕

Create text box link / Previous text box / Next text box / Change text direction

2 Click 🔗 on the Text Box toolbar.

3 Click on the second text box.

Our reason for writing this book is to share our experiences gained over many years of coaching people in a variety of

companies. In this book we present the structure that we use both in coaching our clients and as a basis for teaching coaching to managers and directors.

Break
forward link

To remove the link, click on the frame of the text box with the

link and click on ![icon].

Make text flow sideways

1 In the **Insert** menu, select **Text Box**.

2 Click and drag text box until it is the size that you want.

3 Enter text, and format the text box to your requirements.

4 In the Text Box toolbar, select .

5 Make any other formatting changes.

6 Click outside the text box to deselect it.

Add text to an AutoShape

1 Insert desired AutoShape into your document.

2 Right-click on the AutoShape and select **Add Text**.

3 Enter the text that you want to appear.

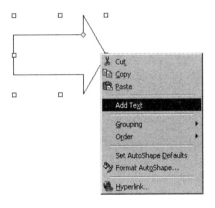

Create a hyperlink to a web page

If you type a web address into a Word document, it will automatically convert it into a hyperlink. You can also create a hyperlink manually, using the text of your choice to appear instead of the web address.

1 Move cursor to where you want your hyperlink to appear.

2 Click on ▆.

3 Type the text that will appear as the hyperlink.

4 You can add a screen tip (caption) if you wish.

5 Type in the web page address or select it from the list of browsed pages.

6 Click **OK**.

> Great free stuff here!

To go straight to my site, click here!

Create a hyperlink to another file or document

1 Move cursor to where you want your hyperlink to appear.

2 Click on 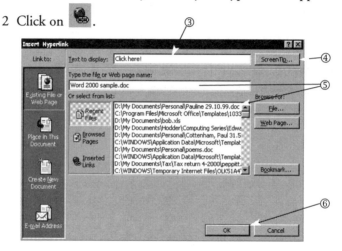.

3 Type the text that will appear as the hyperlink.

4 You can add a screen tip (caption) if you wish.

5 Type in the file path for the document, or select it from the list of recent files.

6 Click **OK**.

Create a basic web page

Word comes pre-loaded with a number of web page templates, as well as a wizard.

1 In the **File** menu, select **New**.

2 Click on **Web Pages** tab.

3 Double-click on the web page template that you want to use.

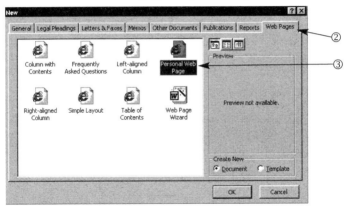

4 Use the template as the basis for your web page.

5 Overwrite the existing copy with your own words.

6 Save your web page.

Save a document as a web page

Ensure that the document works satisfactorily as a web page by seeing what it looks like in Web Layout View first. Click 🖾 .

1 In the **File** menu, select **Save as Web Page**.

2 Navigate to a suitable directory and give your web page a name.

3 Click **Save**.

4 In the **File** menu, select **Web Page Preview** to view the document as a web page.

If Word warns you that converting your document into a web page will lose certain items, you can:

• Continue anyway and accept that the finished web page will not look exactly like the original Word document.

• Cancel the operation, return to Word and modify the document before trying again.

View the HTML source of a web page

1 Open a web page, or a document that has been saved as a web page.

2 In the **View** menu, select **HTML Source**.

3 Make changes to the HTML source code as required.

4 In the **File** menu, select **Exit**.

Styles

Use a style

A style is a collection of formatting characteristics that has been given a name. Applying a style enables you to make several formatting changes in one go.

There are two kinds of styles:

• **Paragraph** styles apply to whole paragraphs. They specify a combination of font, indentation, line spacing, tabs etc.

• **Character** styles define the look of one or more characters, and specify formatting such as font, underlining and bold.

Word comes with several predefined styles, or you can create your own.

View style names

The current style name is displayed in the field at the left of the
Formatting toolbar. The default style name is Normal.

Click on the downward-pointing arrow to right of the **Style
name** to see the list of style names to choose from.

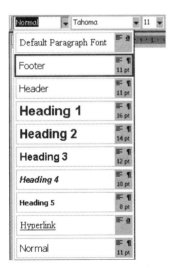

Create a new style

1 In the **Format** menu, select **Style**.

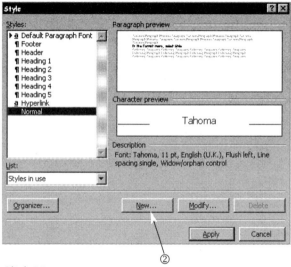

2 Click **New**.

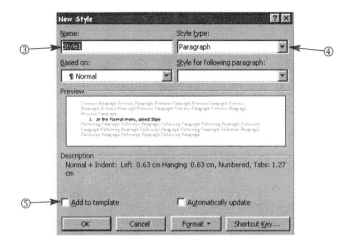

3 Give the style a name.

4 Select a **Style type**.

5 Place a tick in the **Add to template** check box.

6 Click the **Format** button and select **Font**.

7 Select a font style and size.

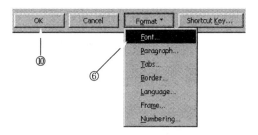

8 Click **OK**.

9 Click again on the format button and repeat steps 6 to 8 for each of the remaining options that are applicable.

10 Click **OK**.

11 Click **Close**.

You will now be able to select the style you have created in the **Style name** drop-down menu.

Apply a style

1 Highlight the paragraph that you want to apply a style to.

2 In the **Style name** drop-down menu, select the style that you want to apply.

Modify a style

1 Apply to any paragraph the style that you want to modify.

2 Make any changes to the formatting of the paragraph.

3 Highlight the whole paragraph.

4 Click in the **Style name** menu.

5 Press **[Enter]**.

6 Click to update the style to reflect recent changes.

7 Click **OK**.

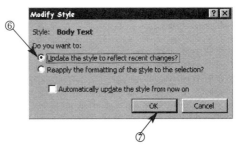

Help Menu

Show the Office Assistant

The Office Assistant is an animated character that sits on your desktop. If the Office Assistant is running, help is available via the character's speech bubble. The Office Assistant will also offer tips and advice based on what you are doing in Word.

You can specify the way in which the Office Assistant provides help.

1 In the **Help** menu, select **Show the Office Assistant**.

2 Click on the **Office Assistant**.

3 Click **Options**.

4 Click on the **Options** tab.

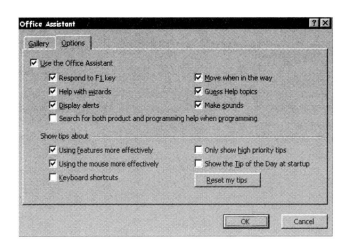

5 Click to select the options you require.

6 Click **OK**.

Use the Office Assistant

1 Click on the Office Assistant.

2 Type a question.

3 Click **Search**.

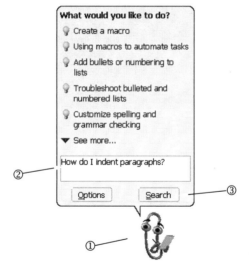

What would you like to do?

- Create a macro
- Using macros to automate tasks
- Add bullets or numbering to lists
- Troubleshoot bulleted and numbered lists
- Customize spelling and grammar checking

▼ See more...

② — How do I indent paragraphs?

[Options]   [Search] — ③

①

4 Select from the range of answers provided.

5 You will now be taken to specific help.

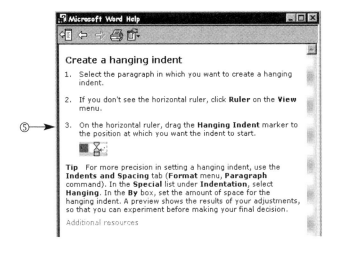

Create a hanging indent

1. Select the paragraph in which you want to create a hanging indent.

2. If you don't see the horizontal ruler, click **Ruler** on the **View** menu.

⑤→ 3. On the horizontal ruler, drag the **Hanging Indent** marker to the position at which you want the indent to start.

Tip   For more precision in setting a hanging indent, use the **Indents and Spacing** tab (**Format** menu, **Paragraph** command). In the **Special** list under **Indentation**, select **Hanging**. In the **By** box, set the amount of space for the hanging indent. A preview shows the results of your adjustments, so that you can experiment before making your final decision.

Additional resources

tip

Try to make your question as precise as you can, otherwise you will not always find the answers you are looking for.

Turn off the Office Assistant

Many users find the Office Assistant irritating, and you may
wish to turn this feature off.

1 Click on the Office Assistant.

2 Click **Options**.

3 Click on the **Options** tab.

4 Click once to remove the tick in **Use the Office Assistant**.

> ### tip
>
> You can also turn off the Office Assistant by right-clicking on
> the Office Assistant and selecting Hide. But if you do this, the
> Office Assistant will return next time you open Word!

Use the What's This? command

1 In the **Help** menu, select **What's This?**

   OR

   Hold down **[Shift]** and press **[F1]**.

2 Mouse pointer will turn into a question mark.

3 Click on any feature within Word for a quick help summary.

For example:

• If you click on text, a caption appears summarizing font and paragraph formatting.

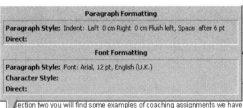

• If you click on a toolbar command, a caption summarizes the command's functionality.

Use the Help command

The Help command is more useful if the Office Assistant is turned off (see above).

1 In the **Help** menu, select **Microsoft Word Help**.

   OR

   Press **[F1]**.

2 Click on the **Contents** tab to see the range of help topics available. Double-click on a topic, select an individual query, and the help will appear in the preview screen on the right of the Help dialog box.

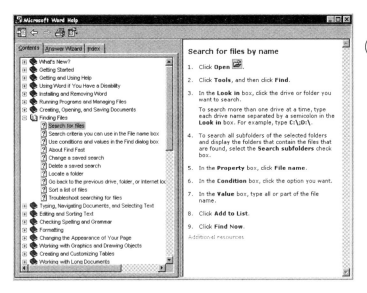

tip

The Help menu is vast, so it is worth persevering in order to find the answer you are looking for.

3 Click on the **Answer Wizard** tab if you have a specific question. Type in the question, click **Search**, then select a topic to display.

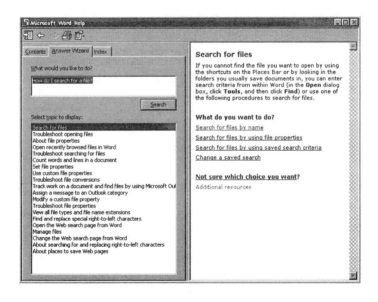

4 Click on the **Index** tab to enter a keyword of your own or to select a keyword from the alphabetical list. Help relating to the keyword will then be displayed.

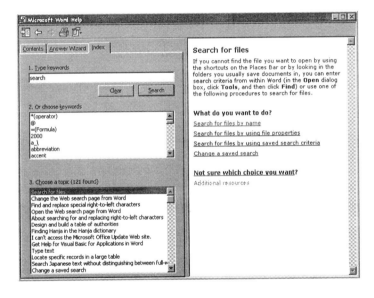

Insert symbols and special characters

1 Move cursor to where you want to insert the symbol or special character.

2 In the **Insert** menu, select **Symbol**.

3 Click on **Symbols** tab.

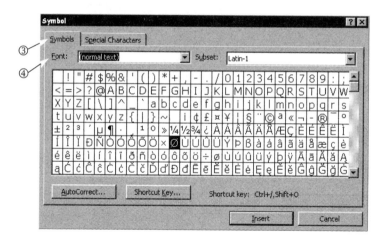

4 Choose an appropriate font.

5 Select the character that you want to use.

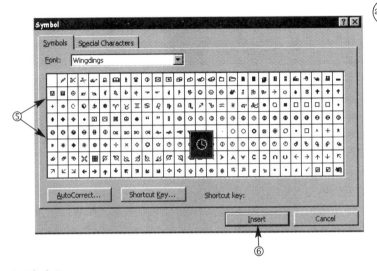

6 Click **Insert**.

1 Open the document that you want to protect.

2 In the **File** menu, select **Save As**.

3 In the **Tools** drop-down menu, in the **Save As** dialog box, click **General Options**.

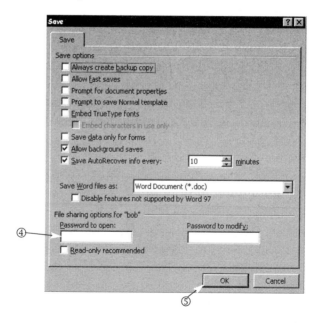

4 Type a password in the **Password to open** box.

5 Click **OK**.

6 Type the password again in the **Re-enter password to open** box.

7 Click **OK**.

8 Click **Save**.

tip

You can also prevent a document from being modified with a password. Repeat steps 1–8 above, but this time enter the password in the 'Password to modify' field.

Switch between imperial and metric measurement

You can change the default unit of measure that Microsoft Word uses for measurements in dialog boxes and rulers.

1 In the **Tools** menu, select **Options**.

2 Click on the **General** tab.

3 In the **Measurement units** box, click the option you want.

4 Click **OK**.

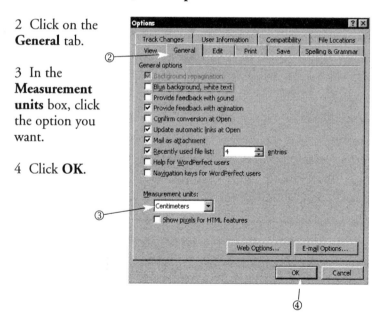

Personalize menus and toolbars

There are a number of ways in which you can customize the menus and toolbars that you use in Word.

1 In the **Tools** menu, select **Customize**.

2 Click on each of the tabs to see the customization options available.

CUSTOMIZE
TOOLBARS

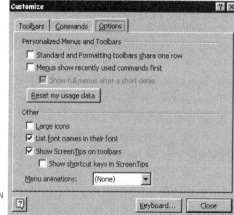

CUSTOMIZE
MENUS

OTHER
CUSTOMIZATION
OPTIONS

Get help from the Web

If you can't find what you are looking for in the **Help** menu, it
might be worth checking out the extra help Microsoft provides
on the Web.

1 Connect to the Internet.

2 In the **Help** menu, select **Office on the Web**.

You can search for more help, downloads and updates.

Change how often Word saves documents automatically

1 In the **Tools** menu, select **Options**.

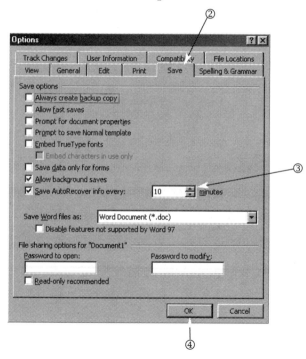

2 Click on the **Save** tab.

3 Adjust the AutoRecovery time where indicated.

4 Click **OK**.

Recover a document that was saved automatically

1 In the **File** menu, select **Open**.

2 Navigate to the folder containing recovered files. This is usually:

   Windows\Application Data\Microsoft\Word

3 Select **All Files** in the **Files of type** drop-down menu.

4 Locate the recovery file and double-click to open it.

5 In the **File** menu, select **Save**.

6 Select the original name for the document.

7 When prompted, agree to replace the existing document.

Let Word create a backup copy of a document

1 In the **File** menu, select **Save As**.

2 Click on **Tools** and select **General Options**.

3 Place a tick in the **Always create backup copy** check box.

4 Click **OK**.

5 Click **Save**.

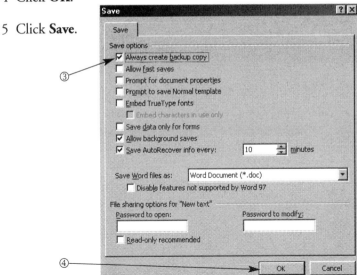

Macros

Use a macro

A macro is a sequence of keystrokes or commands that you have recorded in Word, which you can use to save time and reduce errors.

For example, you can create a macro that:

• Inserts a dropped capital letter in the first word of every paragraph in a document.

• Saves a document and prints it out.

Set up a macro

1 Open the document.

2 In the **Tools** menu, point to **Macro** and select **Record New Macro**.

3 Give the new macro a meaningful name.

4 Give the new macro a description.

5 In the **Store macro in** field, decide whether to make the macro available in all documents based on the Normal template or just the existing document.

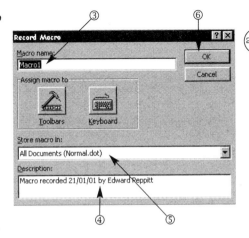

6 Click **OK** to start recording your macro.

Record a macro

1 Perform the operation that you want to create a macro for.

2 When you have finished, click **Stop Recording** on Macro toolbar.

3 In the **Tools** menu, point to **Macro** and select **Macros**.

4 Select the macro you recorded and click **Run**.

Assign a keystroke combination to a macro

1 In the **Tools** menu, select **Customize**.

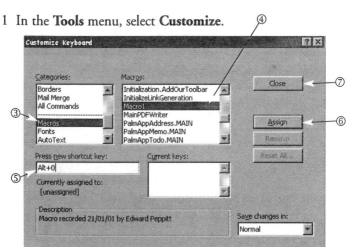

2 Click **Keyboard** button.

3 In the **Categories** box, select **Macros**.

⁣ ct the macro you have recorded.

Ɡn a suitable shortcut.

k **Assign**.

k **Close**.